Humbled ~ Letters From Prison

Dear Father, Forgive Me

by

Jayson Williams

Copyright © 2012 by Jayson Williams

Humbled – Letters From Prison
Dear Father, Forgive Me
by Jayson Williams

Printed in the United States of America

ISBN 9781622304639

All rights reserved solely by the author. The author guarantees all contents are original and do not infringe upon the legal rights of any other person or work. No part of this book may be reproduced in any form without the permission of the author. The views expressed in this book are not necessarily those of the publisher.

Unless otherwise indicated, Bible quotations are taken from the King James Version.

www.xulonpress.com

For

Mommy & Daddy

Linda, Laura

& Ann

Foreword

Dr. DeForest B. Soaries, Jr.

After the tragic shooting incident that took the lives of 14 students and one teacher at Columbine High School in Colorado in April 1999, the governor of New Jersey assigned me the task of organizing a strategy that would minimize the likelihood of our state having a similar experience. I had recently been appointed to the position of New Jersey's Secretary of State to complete the unexpired term of the previous holder of that position. And unlike my peers in other states, I had a very flexible job description. I had a few statutory responsibilities as a constitutional officer of the State. Every time someone filed a lawsuit against the State of New Jersey I was named in the litigation because of my position. My signature was applied to bills that became laws and to certificates of appointment for state officials. But I was appointed by New Jersey's first female governor to help with matters of special concern. Being the mother of teens while she was governor, kids were of special concern. So school violence prevention became a part of my job description.

After meeting with students, school officials and parent organizations, it was clear to me and to my staff that our strategy would need two key elements. First, it had to be led by students. If we were going to have any success with students, their peers would have to be the primary leaders of the effort. We developed a student-led strategy that would empower students to create their own projects that focused on violence, victimization and vandalism. The second element was that we needed a celebrity – someone kids would recognize and respect – to be the spokesperson for the campaign. Everyone familiar with our undertaking agreed rather quickly that there was one person who fit the bill perfectly. And the beauty was that he was not only a real celebrity, but that he lived in New Jersey, worked in New Jersey and had made New Jersey proud. The person unanimously identified for this important role was the professional basketball player and NBA all-star Jayson Williams who played center for the New Jersey Nets. He was the perfect celebrity for our violence prevention campaign.

Fortunately, Jayson had participated in a previous activity with the governor and high-ranking state officials and senior staff in my office had maintained a relationship and contact with him. When they called him and told him what we were doing and how he could assist, he immediately offered to participate in any way he could. I was somewhat skeptical when I received this news. I expected to be referred to a business agent, a manager, a lawyer or some other handler that would function as an intermediary for Jayson. After all, one of the primary needs that famous people have is to hire people who can protect, shield and otherwise be a buffer for them from an adoring and sometimes abusive public. So I was expecting to be asked to jump through at least a few "hoops" to get to this hoops star! It was somewhat amazing that an NBA all-star with a $100 million contract would take a phone call – even from the Secretary of State – and simply say "Come on over!" But that is exactly what happened.

And when I received that news, I remembered a conversation that I had previously with a friend of mine who had assembled a group of investors to purchase the Nets basketball team. This friend had no interest in basketball at all. In fact, I am not sure he ever attended a basketball game in his life. But his interest in buying

Foreword

the Nets was motivated by his commitment to the City of Newark where he had grown up. His strategy was to buy the Nets, move the team to Newark and create a reason for Newark to have a state of the art downtown sports arena that would function as a catalyst for the city's economic revitalization. The profits generated by the team's revenue would help youth serving organizations in the city and the positive impact would be tremendous. When my friend's group completed their acquisition of the Nets, he quickly got to know Jayson. He called me and urged me to get to know Jayson also because in his words Jayson was "the real deal."

And Jayson Williams became our celebrity spokesperson for our violence prevention campaign that aimed at preventing violence, vandalism and victimization. He appeared on a video that we showed to every student leader in the state. He was funny, focused and transparent about the pain that he felt when his sister was a victim of violence and ultimately died. Students reacted visibly when they heard his message. He made a big difference in our efforts. And this was just one of the many philanthropic and civic projects that Jayson Williams supported in his adopted state, New Jersey. In many instances, he not only did volunteer work, but he also donated the funds to pay for the project in which he was volunteering.

I left public office in 2002, one month before the tragic accident at Jayson's house that claimed the life of Mr. Christofi, the chauffer he hired that evening to transport friends and family to dinner after a basketball game. So my official association with the state sponsored violence prevention program had ended. But I knew that Jayson's involvement in violence prevention activities would be overshadowed by the news of this incident for the rest of his life. And I would come to learn that the pain of losing his sisters was just the tip of the Jayson Williams' iceberg of pain that had grown beneath the surface of his contagious smiles and athletic successes.

Now he has finally told his story.

While visiting with Jayson in prison, he thanked me for urging him to finally abandon his legal challenge to his remaining charges and to accept the plea agreement that had been offered by the State in 2010. Initially, I thought that was quite strange. But he has proven to have a deep appreciation for both the opportunity and the challenge of facing himself and starting his life over again – even if it had to occur behind prison bars. In church we call that being "born again." I respect what he has attempted to do.

There are many people who are very skeptical of "jailhouse" religion. A cynic will predictably say that Jayson is simply using religion to position himself in a favorable light once again. And only Jayson knows what his true motives are. But there are two realities that the public and the readers of this book will have to acknowledge. The first is that many jailhouse conversions have been quite legitimate and have really stuck. Convicted Watergate conspirator Chuck Colson participated in one of the worst government crimes this country has ever witnessed. Colson's aid to President Richard Nixon in committing crimes that would compromise the office of the President and embarrass the entire nation resulted in his serving time in a federal prison, a complete reversal of fortune for a man who had unlimited access to presidential power. While in prison, Colson took a look at himself and had a conversion experience that resulted in him becoming an influential Christian leader whose stature rivaled Billy Graham. People were skeptical – but time has answered all questions concerning Colson's conversion.

The second point the skeptics should recognize is that anyone who reveals as much about his life's secrets as Jayson has in this book must be very serious about changing. It is hard enough to admit our weaknesses and reveal our vulnerabilities to ourselves. Many of our personal problems stem from our inability to tell ourselves the truth about ourselves. But when a public figure has been humbled to the point of admitting the truth about himself to the very public from whom he seeks admiration – that is something worth respecting and giving the benefit of the doubt.

There can be no forgiveness where there is no repentance. But when confession and genuine repentance do occur, forgiveness is an appropriate response.

Time will tell whether or not Jayson Williams will accept his new life and use his experience to be a witness to others. He has had previous experience with comebacks from physical injury during his athletic days. This may serve him well as he continues his spiritual comeback and his return to having to make decisions for himself. He has a great role model in a guy who persecuted the Christians and then a dramatic conversion led to his actually building churches. About his potential to remain faithful and focused on his new life, this man said these words: "I can do all things through Christ who strengthens me." Jayson has access to the same Power that St. Paul had when he said those words about himself. And he will have plenty of fans that have taken the same journey and will be cheering for him. And he will have at least one pastor in his corner.

DeForest B. Soaries, Jr.
Senior Pastor
First Baptist Church of Lincoln Gardens
Somerset, New Jersey

"Then you will know the truth, and the TRUTH will set you FREE." John 8:32

Letters

Humbled is a compilation of the journals and letters I wrote during my incarceration.
My heartfelt thanks and appreciation goes out to everyone who supported me, prayed for me, and stood by me in the valley. Your unconditional love and encouragement gave me the strength to face my demons and share my secrets. I remain totally dependent on God, trusting that He will complete the work that He started in me.
May God bless you on your journey.

With love and thanks,
Jayson Williams

Table of Contents

I. ...19

Don't Snap! ~ Who Do You Say That I Am? ~ Keep Me From Evil ~ Devil's Jug ~ Lesson in Humility ~ So I Thought ~ Know Thyself ~ This Side of Heaven ~ Remote Control ~ Secrets ~ Definitions ~ Wrong! ~ Doctor Knows Best ~ World's Tallest Chemist ~ No Strings Attached ~ Roots

II. ...71

Problem Solving ~ Father of the Year ~ Fanatics ~ Will Power ~ Left Behind ~ Selfish Antenna ~ Molasses in Wintertime ~ Snitches Get Stitches ~ Show Me the Baby ~ Work the Land ~ Hand to the Plow ~ Double-Edged Sword ~ Open Your Jacket ~ Compassion ~ Funky Cold Medina ~ Mr. Deuce

III. ...103

Let's Blame the Athletes ~ Mr. Creative ~ Happy Birthday! ~ Cot in My Penthouse ~ Blvd. of Broken Dreams ~ Second Fiddle ~ Empty Seat ~ Purpose ~ House of Order ~ I Can Handle It ~ Sheep & Wolves ~ Rollies for Hep C ~ Man Amongst Boys ~ Fall Back ~ Isolation ~ Yes & No ~ Saggers ~ Mid-State Radio ~ Be Still ~

IV. ...145

Good Morning ~ Yelling Shoes ~ Blowing Smoke ~ God's Giants ~ Bad Bored ~ Tears of a Clown ~ Lie Down ~ Both Sides ~ 40 Men of Folly ~ Crabs in a Basket ~ Your Own ~ Come Back to Prison ~ Sorrow ~ More Grace ~ Back Pocket - Hirelings ~ More Coffee? ~ Chewed Out ~ Comfort Zone Bullies ~ Hit the Bricks

V. ...191

Ignorance Prevails ~ Two Wolves ~ Millstone ~ Happy Labor Day! ~ Mom, Look Who Came to Dinner! ~ Silly Questions ~ Attitude ~ Dump Trucks in Heaven ~ Stand Behind Me, Satan ~ Black & White ~ Vanilla ~ Fan-Jacked ~ Window Gangsta ~ Dr. Gregory ~ Little White Lie

VI. ...227

Heroes & Villains ~ This is My Season ~ Oxymoron ~ Tantrums ~ No Explanations! ~ Like a Child ~ New Jail Smell ~ Let it Rain! ~ Help Wanted ~ Cobwebs & Cables ~ Can't Be Ruined ~ Lessons at Eight ~ In a Puddle ~ Just Do Me ~ Self ~ Down the Ladder ~ Egotistical, But True! ~ Courage

VII. ...283

Men & Boys ~ Save the World ~ Trouble Tree ~ Happy Thanksgiving ~ Up the Ladder ~ Super Mario ~ Hope ~ Cursing ~ Sleep Conversations ~ Let Sydney Sing! ~ Rich or Poor ~ Merry Christmas ~ No Angel ~ Simple Solution ~ Shake it Off! ~ Take Heed~ Do Over ~ Planted

Humbled
Letters from Prison

By
Jayson Williams

Humbled
Letters from Prison

A good scare is worth
more to a man than good **advice**.
~ Edgar Watson Howe,
Country Town Sayings

I.
Don't Snap!
Who Do You Say That I am?
Keep Me From Evil
Devil's Jug
Lesson in Humility
So I Thought
Know Thyself
This Side of Heaven
Remote Control
Secrets
Definitions
Wrong!
Doctor Knows Best
World's Tallest Chemist
No Strings Attached
Roots

Don't Snap!

A few weeks before I came to prison, my friend Joey got all the "gangstas" from our past together to give me advice on jail life. Now these aren't the Sopranos from a TV show, these are the notorious originals—all the fathers of the children I went to high school with in Howard Beach, Queens, New York. They knew I would be all right physically, but they had concerns about my mental well-being.

Truly, the only thing I was uneasy about was being locked in a tight cell. I'm claustrophobic to the fullest. But the gangstas had some advice for me.

"Don't snap! Don't help the underdog. F*** everyone else. F*** them, they shouldn't have done the crime if they can't do the time."

"Don't trust f*****g anyone! No f*****g one. Jay, no f*****g one. This kid's not listening, Sal! Listen, they all are f*****g low lives!"

I consider myself a street-smart person, but prison, like my Maker, is forming me into a complete person.

Not the gangstas. No disrespect to them, but I hung out with them without my parents' knowledge. Everything I did like that always came to light one way or another.

It's still very difficult to watch the underdog lose. But here in prison, instead of watching who's beating up the underdog, I now ask why. Nine times out of ten, the underdog deserves it. This statistic helps me stay out of lockup, because it means that there's really only one time I should be helping the underdog.

As far as trust goes, Sal, that's a lot easier in here. These guys break your heart every single time. But I had to come to prison to learn true human nature. Everything I do and see in here I file away, and then I study it all before I go to bed. I relive my whole day in my big head every night.

I view people I come across in different categories: jury members, defense witnesses, eye witnesses, experts, witnesses for the state, judges, prosecutors, defense lawyers, etc. Since I'm in the system now, I first identify where they belong in my life, if anywhere, and then move on to discerning their selfish ambitions.

When training for an upcoming season in the NBA, there comes a point when you can start to tell that you're getting in shape. I feel the same way about the knowledge I am obtaining here in prison, and I will take it with me to the other side of the barbed-wire fences.

God is a Genius.

Who Do You Say That I Am?

Dear Daddy,

You know I've always been big on loyalty. If anyone needed my help—whether it was my best friend, a high-profile star, or one of our ranch hands or lawyers—I would gladly bust into a burning building wearing gasoline underwear just to save them. Yes, Dad, I came off like a gangsta, but only when it came to people I cared for, which was most of the people I met. You've seen me act like this a few times, when I thought our family was being threatened. What you didn't see happened more than just a few times, and for some pretty insignificant reasons.

Like the time that swindling family from Brooklyn threatened to lame you if you didn't let them haul our garbage from our restaurants. You never told me because I was a fool. But Shawn told me.

You know I can't stand me a bully. So I called Patrick and told him I had a check for him for the garbage. When he showed up, I took him outside before you could stop me and did him some bodily harm on the curb in front of our bar. You heard the commotion and came running out. I watched you pick up every one of his shattered teeth and I will never forget the look on your face. You were completely disappointed in me! Forgive me, Daddy.

After helping Patrick, your first reaction was to get me out of the neighborhood. Once the coast was clear, I think you realized that just as you had taught me to lay bricks, someone else had taught me how to "curb" a man's teeth. And with my confidence and technique, I did it often. But that doesn't make me a gangsta. It makes me a coward.

Dad, I've seen you shoot three different people on three different occasions. The difference was that you were protecting us—my white mother and your mulatto son. You had no choice.

I know you remember back when I found myself right in the middle of two feuding New York City crime families. My loyalty to certain people—including my high school buddies—almost got me killed and it was only my NBA status that saved me. Or so I thought. God was protecting me even then. Besides, my NBA status was only a façade when alcohol and fighting were imminent.

Daddy, when I went to Riker's Island Prison this week to face my DWI charge, one of the COs snuck me into the gym where a riot broke out. The inmates seemed excited to see me and must have heard I was in the building. Once I was fully inside the gym, they swarmed me like ants on a jelly doughnut. There must have been over 300 of them. Within seconds a "Red Code" sounded, and in 10 seconds, everyone but me was lying face down on the floor.

I immediately tried to help calm the inmates so nobody else would get in trouble. As I told them to do as they were being instructed by the COs with rubber bullets, something terrible happened.

Inmates began whispering to me about all the people I hurt in the streets. And I'm not talking about a few inmates, Daddy. There were at least 30 of them!

"That's a real Nigga! He will do you just as much as look at you if you f*** with him." Similar stories quickly spread throughout the gym, and pretty soon the echoes of, "I can top that Jayson Williams story," were almost too much to bear. I felt dirty, filthy, and ashamed. I was known among my peers as a gangsta, not a philanthropist, not a Christian, not an NBA All-Star, not even a son or a father—a stinkin' gangsta! This is the consensus!

Thugs believe I'm a killer. You will never see anyone in prison "try me" because I outrank every top gang member just by my affiliations with all gangs. And if you wrong me or someone I love, I will put the same effort and dedication that I put into being one of the best rebounding players in the NBA into damaging everything and everybody.

See Daddy, I feel scared and anxious as I write this. And whenever that happens I stop writing. I wonder if I should even bother saying what God has probably already told you over a cup of coffee.

But you know it's in my nature to protect. Whether it's something as simple as my reputation or worse, mistreating someone I love, I will rain down destruction on a bully. At this prison, you don't have to like me, but treat me the way I treat you. If not, let's not interact. I have never liked phones or computers because I'm two phone calls away from anyone in the world, and if someone I love is harmed, I have no time to think. Just dial and damage will come just as sure as the sun will come in the morning. But the common denominator was always alcohol and the company I kept.

Well, there's no alcohol here and I only hang out with one person and he's a Christian. I'm a Christian, too, although I did gangsta-type stuff and didn't always act like one. But I am one and always will be.

I refuse to say that your name is damaged, Daddy. I may have done what they said I've done, but I no longer have to *be* who they think I am. All that really matters is what God thinks of me and what you think of me.

So Daddy, who do *you* say that I am?

Love You Mr. Williams,
Jayson

Keep Me From Evil

I awake here in prison and look at the steel bars on the doors of my new prison home. I almost always think, *Why did I cause so much pain?*
Then, *Why am I in so much pain?*

I roll the opposite way on my bunk and stare at the wall and pray, Oh Lord, keep me from evil, that I may cause no more pain.

I used to "have to" wake up every morning at 6 a.m. in New Jersey. Every morning my daddy would roll up in his pick-up truck then we would head down to our 4-wheeler ATV's to feed horses, sheep, goats, chickens, turkeys, ostriches, cows, pigs, peacocks, and rabbits. Oh how I yearn for the smell of my daddy's cigar and black coffee these days.

My dad didn't care if we were playing the Chicago Bulls in eight hours. This was our routine—no matter what. I had to count the animals, each and every one, and report the count back to him only to hear, "Count 'em again! We should have 164 chickens." After a long night of partying, I was never pleased to do a recount.

See, my dad knew me. He knew how easily I would let the devil into my life when the sun became tired. My dad created this routine so I would stay committed to what we needed as a family and so he could analyze whether I'd been living on the straight and narrow the night before. I didn't want to come home at 3 a.m. and then have to count 800 moving, noisy animals three hours later, and sometimes count them three times.

When I could no longer play basketball due to my injury, I remember the look on my dad's face. It wasn't the look of a father watching his son ride off into the sunset with a $100-million guaranteed contract. I saw only fear in his eyes. It was the look of, *My son no longer has a commitment.*

With no commitment, no routine, and many more late nights to help speed up my demise, my dad was hurried to be with the Lord— by his own son's follies. I gave my dad two strokes, sold the New Jersey farm, had the accident, and moved to South Carolina. God then paralyzed my dad and took his speech. So now with a half-hearted routine, still no commitment, and no voice each day to tell me whether or not my count was sharp, I knew it was only a matter of time. My dad used to say, "A lifetime of happiness as you know it Jayson, no man alive could bear it. It would be hell on earth."

You have to stay with your morning routine, Jayson, I say to myself here in prison. I've always been a guy who works extremely hard in anything I'm committed to. And if I can get my routine correct and purposeful, I will make my dad happy again.

My dad understood me at an early age. He knew I needed belonging, worth, and a sense of competency. He didn't need me to count those animals, he just told me he couldn't do it without me. "It's a three-man job," he would snarl, whenever I suggested his way was redundant. "Me, you, and God. We will be here every morning because when we rest, we rust."

So here in prison, I'm back at my routine and commitment, but I just can't stop thinking I have come too late into a world too old. And now I must learn to control my evil. A man of my stature and influence, and with the ability to put funds in any or all of these evildoers' commissary accounts, I can become the most dangerous man the DOC has ever shown hospitality to. My Lord, the chaos I could cause; the havoc I could wreak; the destruction I could bring.

Oh, Lord, keep me from evil, that I may cause no more pain.

The Devil's Jug

The first time my dad ever saw me drink alcohol was when I was 21 years old. I brought him to the White Horse Tavern in New York City. I ordered him a Johnnie Walker Black and an Absolut and OJ for me. I had just purchased my mom and dad matching Jaguars and a brand new mansion in Cherry Hill, so I was feeling mature.

After a few drinks, my father saw my attitude change and he asked me what I was drinking. He was almost timid, but at the same time hopeful for the answer he wanted to hear. I took a chance because I had the courage of alcohol on my side and answered, "Dad, didn't you hear me say Absolut and OJ?" My dad looked like someone had just pulled a pistol to his temple and said, "I thought you meant all you wanted was *absolutely* orange juice."

His expression then turned to that look he would give me when I was a kid and he told me I couldn't sleep over my friend's house. I remember giving my dad the keys to the new cars and house and he just left them right on the table.

See, my dad knew that alcohol, our family history, and my personality were a terrible mix, and he left the tavern as if someone had just lit the fuse to the bomb. He was right!! You add alcohol and bad company together and I shall become a friend of Satan. Poor decisions are also our cousins.

I have been sober for over 200 days now and one could argue it's because alcohol is unavailable here in prison. Wrong! And for the most part, I'm still around poor company as 90 percent of these inmates have poor self-esteem and drink from the Devil's Jug. But I take it day by day now. I haven't convinced myself yet that upon my release I will never drink again, but I honestly know that the company I keep, places I go, and the decisions I make will never be affected by alcohol again!! Simply put, my self-esteem has returned, along with wanting to act responsibly.

The prayer of Jabez says, "Keep me from my evil and let me cause no more pain." Just imagine how much pain I caused my dad. He had to sit back and watch his son, who now belongs to the "world," self-destruct. You can only tell your son the stove is hot so many times. He has to explore and learn it for himself. Dad, you were right. The stove will hurt me. I won't touch it anymore.

Lesson in Humility

I wrote about one of my earliest lessons in humility in my first book, Loose Balls:

My mom and dad took me down to South Carolina when I was just finishing first grade, and we stayed there for three years. My dad was always a strict disciplinarian, but some of the worst trouble I ever got in, and some of the biggest lessons I ever learned, happened down South. If I'm tough, my years in South Carolina helped make me that way.

Once when I was at school, I was doodling on a piece of homework paper. I swear I'm not exactly sure how it happened, but what came out was a picture of a billy goat with my teacher's face on it. My father used to check my homework every night at the dinner table, and this night he checks, and sees the billy goat drawing.

"What are you trying to do?" he asks. "Make fun of your teacher?"

"No, Dad," I say. "I don't know it happened. I was just doodling."

But he calls up my teacher. In South Carolina, back then, parents knew all the teachers.

"Miss S———," he says, "is my son doing all right in

Lesson In Humility

school?"

"No, sir, Mr. Williams, he is not," she says. Miss S——is an old white lady. And I'm listening, and I'm thinking, Uh-oh!

When my father gets off the phone he turns to me and says, "Well, I'll be up there in the morning to the schoolhouse. And I have to pay a visit to your brother Stacey's classroom, too, because he's been acting up as well."

See, in South Carolina you used to get a beating in school. The teachers were allowed to beat you. And you know what? Sometimes the teachers used to make you beat each other. Like if you both got caught talking, the teacher might make you beat your friend's butt. And if you take it easy on him, the teacher'll beat your butt. So life for a fourth grader in Ritter, South Carolina, was no picnic. But now I was going to have to face something worse than the usual teacher whipping.

That next morning my father wakes up and says, "I'll be at the schoolhouse. You go ahead."

"Oh, Daddy," I say, "please, don't. Don't, Daddy."

He says one word. "Boy," he says. And that's enough. My father would never raise his voice. But he got his message across.

So I'm sitting at my desk, and I know he's coming at about nine o'clock. And sure enough, right at nine, there's a loud knock on the classroom door. Scariest sound I ever heard. It's the principal, and he comes in and he says, "Miss S——, Jayson Williams' father would like to talk to his son in front of the whole class."

My father gets up there and he says, "Now, boys and girls, I want you to know I love my son. But sometimes he thinks he's just a clown in front of you all. So I'm going to do something today to teach him he isn't a clown."

All my classmates are all goggle-eyed. And then my father says, "And for the rest of you who think you're clowns, some of your parents should do the same thing I'm doing today."

Then he tells me to come up there, and he says, "I'm going to teach you what humility is today." And he whips my butt. And I try to crawl through his legs to the door, and he catches my head between his legs and just tore my butt up. Sore for days.

And now he's going to the classroom next door, to get my brother Stacey. And Stacey sees him coming in the door and he jumps out the window and runs home. Stacey wasn't living with us; he was living with his mom, my dad's first wife. So he's safe that night. But Stacey ends up getting a lot worse.

Because that Sunday, while we're playing baseball—that was the only thing to do in Ritter on Sunday, and all 600 people in the town would come watch—Stacey's at third base, waiting for a ground ball. And all of a sudden here comes my father's '73 Thunderbird, with his license plates that said '.45 Magnum.' He comes tearing through the parking lot, spins around, he jumps out and catches Stacey at third base. Whips his butt in front of 600 people.

And that was my dad's way of teaching me how to be humble.

So I Thought

Dear Daddy,

Do you remember what we were doing the day before the accident? I do! And I know you do, too, because I imagine, like me, you kept replaying it in your head to see what you could have done differently to prevent it. Please don't beat yourself up over my carelessness.

It just goes to show you how quickly life can change. One minute everything is good, and then one stupid choice, one terrible decision, and you're blindsided by a tragedy that changes everything.

And now, with all the time in the world to think, I keep going back to that day. There I was—hours away from tragedy—-fooling around with a tractor-trailer and thinking it was funny. Why did I always push things to the limit?

February 13, 2002

I remember waking up at 5:20 a.m., getting out of the bathtub, and throwing on my construction clothes before I headed down to the barn to feed the animals with you. We exchanged our usual good mornings and then immediately got to work throwing the bales of hay and 100 lb. bags of feed onto the back of the tractor.

Four other workers were helping us, including Alfonso, Oscar, and Primo—three brothers from Mexico. Alfonso was the only one who spoke English really well so he would translate for his brothers. They would always anticipate your early morning anecdotes, maybe because they were funny, but I truly believe they just loved to see our family bond. The other worker was Scott, whose real name was actually Fred. Dad, you called him Scott because he was from Scotch Plains, New Jersey. Close enough. Heck, he only worked for us for 31 years.

Scott, who went to be with the Lord in 2008, always gave me his own sobriety test each morning. He knew we would be working with heavy machinery and didn't want to be run over again. Well, that's another story. But he would try to get a sense of my well being by trying to figure out what I did the night before. Of course, you were always interested in my folly, so you co-signed all the questioning.

"What did you and that pretty wife of yours do last night?" Scott asked with an investigating smile. "And how much wine did you have doing it?"

"She didn't come home last night," I said as I threw

the last bag of feed onto the trailer. In an attempt to keep the mood light, you jumped right in with, "Jay's wife Sonya (you could never get her name right—it's *Tanya*) ain't home because she stayed in New York City." Then you told one of your jokes, (and of course, changed the names to Jay and Sonya to make it funnier) and when you delivered the punch line without cracking a smile, we all busted out laughing. And once Alfonso finished translating for his brothers, we enjoyed a laugh a second time.

"Okay, Jay, you and Scott load up the tractor-trailer and move the 15-ton John Deere excavator over to Plainfield." Not the news Scott wanted to hear. At his age, and knowing me since I was an infant, he didn't enjoy driving tractor-trailers with me. He enjoyed me, but not my driving.

"Darn," Scott muttered.

I always seemed to enjoy Scott's reservations about my driving and purposely turned a blind eye to it. It always made it funnier that way, like Mr. Magoo.

Scott drove the track hoe onto the trailer and I began chaining it down. Once we were loaded up, we climbed into the brand new cab-over-engine Freightliner and started the engine. As I pulled off, I wanted to do a quick check to make sure the chains were secure so I slammed on the brakes and dove out of the cab. Sure enough, the chains didn't come loose so were good to go. One quick leap and I was back behind the wheel to find Scott still out of breath from his initial climb. Or maybe it was his nervousness. Despite my 17 years of Class-A commercial driving skills, he still didn't feel comfortable because of my hurry–up-to-wait mentality.

As I maneuvered the tractor-trailer onto the highway with, of course, Scott's backseat driving directing me, I was determined to shift all 18 gears, necessary or not, just to see that look on Scott's face.

I remember my cell phone rang and it was my lawyer,

Sal. He said something about my driver's license being expired (he was incorrect) and Scott overheard and sat up in his seat like he just hit the Lotto. See, Dad, as we know, nothing improves my driving like an expired driver's license.

The next phone call was from my agent, asking me if I would like to go to Harlem the following weekend and have lunch with former president Bill Clinton. "Of course," I answered, glancing proudly at Scott, assuming he was ear hustling this conversation, also. Scott, never missing an opportunity to get me out of the tractor-trailer driving business, quickly suggested, "Why don't you ask President Clinton to help you run for president so I won't have to ride with you anymore?"

Acting confused, I up-shifted to get more speed and just to see that look of distress again. As he whispered prayers for deliverance, I kept thinking how blessed I was to have wealth and fame, knowing I was only enjoying myself this much because it was my hobby, not my actual job.

Scott, noticing my overconfidence and speed, decided to play you, Dad, and said with a sigh, "Wealth is like sea water, the more you drink, the thirstier you become; and the same is true of fame." Might as well take shots at me, since I was out of gears and he was certain we were going to die in a fiery crash anyway. I responded with a nod of, "Whatever."

The phone rang again and this time it was St. John's University, thanking me for my generous donation. Convinced the end was near, and since he was already on a roll, Scott hit me again, "A candle lights others and consumes itself, also."

With no more gears to put him in his place, I just looked over at him for a while, not looking at the road, knowing how uncomfortable this made him. This is where he would typically begin squinting out the windshield in amazement, like he saw Jesus on the hood of

So I Thought

the truck, anything to bring my attention back to the road.

Not this time though. He just stared back at me until I had to lose the contest because our exit was approaching.

After conquering the sharp jug-handle exit, and knowing I wouldn't be able to scare him with high gears for a while because we were within city limits, I fired back with my interpretation of the Bible instead.

"The Bible says that he who lends to the poor gets his interest from God."

Scott, already cocked and loaded, immediately shot back, "The Bible also says a fool and his money will soon part. You just gave two million dollars to the Catholic Church. They ain't poor, fool!"

Before I had a chance to respond, the phone rang again. It was my grandchildren who call me "Uncle Jay."

"Can you take us to see the Globetrotters play tonight?" Alex asked.

Not even checking with Sonya—I mean Tanya, I responded, "Of course I will take you." Scott, smiling like the cat that swallowed the canary, added his two cents, "You know, your wife will eventually come home and tomorrow is Valentine's Day!"

We arrived at the excavator's destination, forcing us to put our war of words on hold. We quickly unloaded the track hoe and then jumped back in the cab to retrieve another, much to Scott's dismay. At this pace we were looking at completing four moves instead of two and doubling his odds of dying in a fiery crash.

As we left and started heading down Watchung Ave., a two-lane county road, a car suddenly stopped in front of me. No way I could have stopped in time so I had to go right. Now Dad, you know I had to exaggerate my right turn just to clear the trailer from running over the car. So as I jerked the steering wheel all the way to the right, it "appeared" as though I was headed straight for a glass-enclosed bus station with about nine people inside. Now, when they saw this truck that "appeared" to be coming to squash them, they all began to scatter like roaches exposed to sudden light. One problem: they were all trapped in the glass-enclosed shelter.

So as some patrons dropped their phones and threw their newspapers, and others tried to climb the back wall, I just turned the steering wheel back to the left, glancing in my left side view mirror to admire how I cleared that car at 35 mph. Not Scott. He was bright-eyed and screaming, looking in his right side view mirror. His mirror showed newspapers flying while some people were cursing and others were praying. One Puerto Rican guy was so mad he was chasing after the truck, yelling and grabbing his privates.

As I turned onto Highway 78, knowing that that was definitely a close one, I decided to upshift less aggressively so I wouldn't scare Scott any more than I already had. Finally, Scott was out of clichés, and even though I wasn't out of gears, I chose not to use them because of the Buckwheat expression of fear on his face. I wouldn't give him the satisfaction of catching eyes, but let me tell you this, I practically bit a hole in my lip holding back my laughter because Scott stared at me non-stop for 40 minutes straight—all the way home.

Dad, I had only two thoughts: 1) *Scott is still staring at me*, and 2) *life is so good!*

So I thought.

J

Know Thyself

Dear Dad,

It's 5:48 a.m. and I just finished my morning workout, then showered and made the bed (literally) that I must lie in. I showed a couple of inmates my journal yesterday. One said, "Man, you are a little hard on yourself." Another said, "I don't think I would ever write that down on paper for people to see." Well I did write it down and no way am I being hard on myself.

> Know thyself?
>
> If I knew myself,
>
> I'd run away.

Exactly! That says it all. I am in prison not only for my latest conviction, but for the hundreds I didn't get convicted on. I can't sugarcoat my charges. A man died because of me, although it was an accident. But then I tried to cover it up like a coward. I wasn't a child, I was "the man."

Inmates often say to me, "Jay, you don't belong here man. I can tell just by talking to you." What this inmate doesn't know is that if you make people in here *think* they're thinking, they'll love you. If you *really* make them think, they'll hate you.

I'm where I'm supposed to be and when I'm supposed to be here.

People try to patronize me with fake pity saying, "Ah, man, sorry about that bad article in the paper about you." I reply, "Well they *are* keeping me alive. Plus, they wrap dead fish with newspapers."

God loves me so much that He put me in an incubator where He can slowly protect and reform me.

Miss you,
Jayson

This Side of Heaven

Linda, once radiant, weighed only 70 pounds in

his mother die of AIDS in 1993. Jay bid aunt Laura farewell five years later.

Dear God,

You took three of my sisters from me: Linda and Laura died from AIDS, and Ann was shot in the face by her own husband. I always thought You gave me the wealth and fame to make up for taking the people I loved and for screwing up my life with tragedy upon tragedy. Now we're even, I would tell You.

I remember walking home from school that day in June. I could see a crowd in front of her apartment building. She lived across the street from us on Cherry Street in New York

City. I remember pushing my way through to get to the front entrance and then I just remember seeing the blood. There was all kind of blood everywhere, on the floor and walls, and by the elevator—it was like a pathway of blood leading all the way to my sister's door.

And right away, just inside her door I see Ejay. And he's just a baby—maybe a year and a half old. And he's hysterical. Just crying and stumbling around the living room, all covered in his mommy's blood.

The next thing I remember is turning the corner and there was Linda, my oldest sister, just lying there in the bathtub in a shallow pool of blood.

I was shouting for somebody to do something. Mom was calling someone on the phone while trying to talk to my sister. I ran to her kitchen and grabbed a knife. And here I am, a little 12-year-old kid, hunting for this coward, room after room, daring him to show his face.

My sister managed to whisper to me that he had blood on his sneakers and then she went fully unconscious. As soon as she said that, I tore out of that place and raced down the street to the park. And I just knew I was gonna find this monster that hurt her like that. And there I stood in the middle of the park, me and my knife. I just kept looking at everyone's feet, looking for blood. I was looking for anyone with blood on his shoes.

You spared her life, God, but let the doctors pump her veins full of poison? Why let her survive in the first place? You knew she would leave the hospital with a virus that would destroy both my sisters, and life as we knew it. Things were never the same after that. We were all living the nightmare, one that only happens to people on TV, or in the movies. How can you go from living life to living torment in less than 24 hours? If You are so powerful, if You are in charge—how does this happen?

"I dare you," I would pray. "Come on, God. Do it." I wanted You to take me, too, so I could see my sisters again. I remember so many late nights during my early years in the NBA. I would come back to my apartment and watch TV till I couldn't keep my eyes open anymore and then try to sleep as long as possible just in case they might visit me in my dreams.

Everywhere that Sergio cut her she began to scar, and I hated him for that. That monster cut up my beautiful sister and beat her with a hammer for two dollars! Two worthless dollars was all he found in her purse. He destroyed her, and everyone who loved her. He stole something she could never get back. And You never stopped him. She was, and still is, the most beautiful woman I have ever known.

He only got six years for that crime and You know what? Forgive me for this, but I waited. I waited and my friends waited. When he got out of prison, we were there. We caught up to him in the neighborhood and we took him to the park and I hit him and hit him and hit him until he was red with blood. One of my friends gave me a gun and said, "Finish him off, Jay. Square things now, for you and your sisters."

My friends walked away and left me with some privacy. It was just me, this man, the gun, and You. I pressed that gun right into the eye of the man who killed my sister, my sisters, and for some reason, I couldn't do it. I considered myself strong and tough, but I just couldn't bring myself to pull the trigger. You wouldn't let me do it. Had my friends stayed, I would have done it, God.

I can still see his face, his eyes pleading with me in distress. He was sweating, shaking, crying so much, and begging for his life.

"You did a bad thing," I said.

"I know, I know," he said, crying.

I told him, "You better run as fast as you can, because if my boys see you alive, they won't be like me. They will kill you!" I hit him one more time on the head with the butt of the pistol, and then cut him loose and let him go.

He sprinted out of there. Never even looked back once. And that was the last I saw of him. I still think about that sometimes and I still think about him. But I think about my sisters every single day.

It took a terrible tragedy for me to sit in prison and realize that I have nothing. The money, cars, jewelry, houses, things, and all that time—none of it was ever mine. It all belonged to You. Even my sisters. Everything is Yours, God, and You give and You take as You see fit, and sometimes for reasons we will never understand this side of Heaven.

J

Remote Control

I can see the TV from my bunk here in the prison, but I can't hear it. Just a few months ago when I was hooked on TV like a jacket on a coat hook, this would've been a small emergency. "I can't hear the TV! Where's the remote?!" I would have my wife and kids stop whatever they were doing and find the remote so I could hear the TV. Wow, how God knows my vices.

God knew I couldn't watch six hours of TV and spend five minutes reading my Bible and grow closer to Him. So something I took for granted (the Bible, not the TV) is now my #1 priority. Again! God said I should keep it with me all the time and read it every day of my life. Wow. God sure goes a long way just to get me to read my Bible. (LOL)

Secrets

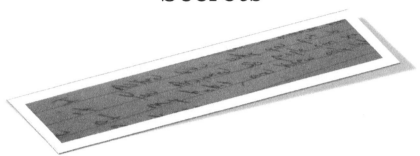

Dear Dad,

Hold on to Jesus for this one. I never thought you and I would ever have this conversation and I guess there's no other way to say it so here goes...

I recreationally used a stimulant, Daddy. Not every day, or even every week, but it was situational and typically at the end of the night. I'm ashamed to tell you of this particular failure, but for me to be free of and resistant to the darkness that seasonally entered my life, I must confess, and then repent.

There, it's done! I will work with everything in my power not to leave the narrow road to Eternity again! Any man may make a mistake, none but a fool will stick to it. I'm no longer filled with folly and now that I'm isolated, I've asked God to help me figure out with whom, where, and why I danced with the devil.

Dad, I would like to say that I only used this with people I just randomly met. Not true. About 90 percent of my circle before the accident were users, including family members. You are now in Heaven Dad, and you have the biggest television with unlimited realities to break your heart. So I don't have to tell you who the guilty parties are, you know. You also know that for many months "it" has knocked at my door, but just like a Mormon salesman, I run from it.

See Dad, this stimulant is used for longevity in alcohol abuse and I have never used it without alcohol. I wanted to keep drinking, most of the time because I didn't like who I was or who I was with. Right when you think your equilibrium can't stand anymore, here comes a stimulant that screams, "Don't put that coat on yet, I will balance you out!" So I would keep on drinking to the point where I couldn't taste the bitterness in the alcohol anymore.

Pretty soon, Dad, the party has been reincarnated and has moved from the bar to my home. See, this stimulant makes you so paranoid that you must get to a comfortable location or you will wear out a set of eyeballs and a neck just being on the lookout. At times, believe it or not, hiding the habit and not letting anyone else see you do it was part of being in this secret society. Anyone could tell you were on it, but only the privileged few were actually allowed to see you use it, or even partake themselves. The key word being "secret," Dad. It was like I had two kinds of secrets when using: one was not worth keeping and the other was too good to keep.

This stimulant usually makes its first appearance around 2 a.m.—you inhale and then chase the first consumption in vain all night long. As the morning becomes afternoon, the secret society is no longer a secret and just about anyone with the same intentions is allowed membership. Alcohol and the stimulant! Two wrongs don't make a right, but together they made a heck of an excuse.

By this point, I had let my guard down and my worst desires became attainable because I could no longer reason and had the ultimate excuse— *I was high.* I can't speak for anyone else but me, but let me tell you that you can end up just short of a pornographic movie, or even worse, tell things that should never leave your soul. The high is unpredictable and for me, was very rarely premeditated.

It's my fault, Dad. I chose the company I kept. He that lies down with dogs will rise up with fleas. And the fleas don't have to be the ones who were with me at the time of consumption; they can be with me as I arrive at my final destination and neglect to check me on this issue, because then they would be citing hypocrisy.

This stimulant was the worst host that insisted on introducing me to the people with the lowest self-esteem ever. The most important thing I have to do starting right now is watch the company I keep. I can't make a crab walk straight. And just like Mark Twain said, "The measure of a man's real character is what he would do if he knew he would never be found out." No mistakes anymore, just lessons. No more bloody noses and hang-overs. I'm just saying I did it and I won't do it again. It's that simple, Dad. I won't apologize. I will flee this vice and will once again make you happy with me.

Dad, I remember when we built my house in West New Jersey, I asked you why you put so many windows in it. You answered, "So people can see inside." You knew of my habit, and knew only light could take me out of the darkness.

Forgive me,
Jayson

Definitions

Dear Dad,

Today is my ex-wife's and my anniversary. I knew my children's mother for 20 years and was married to her for eight—no nine, no eight...heck, I don't even remember—but what I do remember are the words this beautiful young lady always used to describe me! Since I'm in prison and have a little extra time on my hands, I thought I would look them up in the dictionary and see if I agree with her.

Selfish: *concerned chiefly or only with oneself.*

Hmmm, now I have a two-part response to this particular adjective. I have never been selfish monetarily. This is evident in the luxurious lifestyle we live. So, *no* to the first part. But I was selfish with my time. My children didn't care about or know the value of money. But they did know that their daddy wasn't there. With me being retired, there was no excuse for that. I went out on the town to escape the debt I owed to society. I selfishly chose a night on the town over tucking my kids in to sleep. Now that's the ultimate selfishness.

Now on to the next word: *egotistic—(Son of a *****).*

Well, let's just look up the former.

Egotistic: *a selfish, self-centered person.*

Starting to see a pattern here. There goes that word *selfish* again. But we already dealt with that. Let's just deal with self-centered. "Amen."

When I was 11 years old, a couple of buddies and I saw UCLA play on TV. I immediately announced that I was going to play for that school. Nobody believed me, but me. One of my friends said, "You can't even make our little league team."

That was the day I thought I lied to my friends and myself. So I bragged to anyone who would listen about how great I was in basketball. Turns out I am. So I am also self-centered. That comes with the territory. If you don't agree with me, you were never great. And that's okay, too.

Moving on to another one of her favorites.

Reckless*: showing no regard for danger or consequences.*

Self-explanatory—I'm in prison, Dad. Enough said!

And finally, a word that has also been on my mind lately...

Closure: *the act of closing or the state of being closed; a bringing to an end, a conclusion.*

Yes, I agree with this *cold*heartedly. I have a good heart, but that's not the full package. You need to raise a family the right way. I sometimes egotistically and selfishly (and at the incorrect time and with the wrong company) would shout, "I have done everything a man is supposed to do and not supposed to do!" Believe it or not, a few years ago, I would only tolerate being the top of the top, and now (according to some), I'm the top of the bottom!

My ex-wife and children did not leave me. I left them

Definitions

the day I became a selfish, egotistical, reckless man.

Love,
J

P.S. Gathered at the Passover feast...Jesus took a towel and basin and *redefined* greatness. ~ Richard C. Foster, *The Celebration of Discipline*

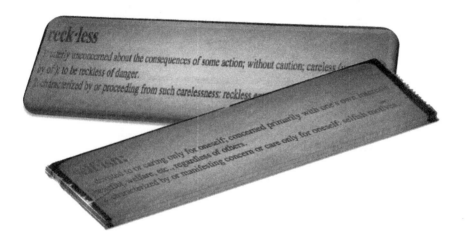

Wrong!

Dear Dad,

C.R.A.F. (Central Reception and Assignment Facility) is where all inmates go after sentencing to await transfer to their assigned prison. Depending on how things go, you could be there for anywhere from a few days to a few months, or longer. All I know is my first five minutes there went terribly wrong.

A well-seasoned inmate greeted me, then went straight into giving advice.

"Look brother, you don't tell me where my cell is! Let the corrections officer tell me where my cell is! You dig?!" It was my best new prison voice, followed by a head snap to the side.

Without looking up, the CO called out from behind his clipboard, "That *is* your cell, Williams."

With an apathetic shrug, I turned on my heel and slid past the barred gate, only to be jolted from my pimp strut and slammed up against the wall of the steel cage by a squad of COs wearing riot gear.

I was ordered to strip naked, along with five of my new acquaintances, and then ushered into a larger holding cell. Sitting naked and frozen on the concrete floor, (Dad, hear me: *naked and frozen on the concrete floor!*), I thought to myself: *It don't get any worse than this.*

WRONG!

"Amigo Negro? Tu hablas Español?" A small Puerto Rican gang member asks me, scoping the vicinity for guards.

"Nah man, I don't speak no Spañol!" I say as aggressively as possible without moving my lips. I figured the language barrier would kill our conversation for the rest of this adventure.

WRONG!

The Puerto Rican gang member is persistent and asks again, "Black Brotha', can you pass something over to the other papi next to you?"

Like a ventriloquist, I whisper, "Are you crazy man!? They are watching."

For the next four minutes, the conversation went something like this:

"Por favor, Negro?"

"Heck NO, Chico!"

"Por favor, my friend?"

"No way, my dude!"

Finally, the CO turned his back and the coast was clear, so I agreed to a quick transfer, thinking I better get some jail credits, or whatever they call it, for this.

"Come on, Chico, pass it." I muttered, facing the opposite direction from where he was squatting. "Hurry up, Jose!" I urged.

"How did you know my name is Jose, Negro? You

un policia?"

"No man. Lucky guess." As I slowly turned to face him, I was horrified to see him squatting with what looked like his wrist up his butt. Frozen and wide-eyed, I just kept staring, then jerked my eyes upward to find him staring back at me.

"Here Leroy," Jose says to me, now speaking perfect English. "Pass this over to the other Jose," he says sarcastically as he tries to hand me something.

"Man, you gotta be out ya crazy mind if you think I'm gonna pass whatever it is that you just dug out from your butt," I whisper yelled, dipping to avoid his outstretched arm. "I ain't touching that!" Now I'm *hoping* the cameras are watching. "I'll lean forward and then you can pass it over, but no way on God's green earth am I touchin' whatever it is you just pulled out of you. Throw it!"

So Jose threw it behind me, and considering where it came from, I didn't expect to hear any noise when it hit the floor.

WRONG!

Clang! Clang! Clang! It bounced off of my back, onto the floor, and then landed half on the other Jose's foot. I have a good imagination, but couldn't even begin to figure this one out. I turned around and there it was in all its glory— a cell phone. Yep! A cell phone!

"You can use it when we get back to the cell," the other Jose offered, scooping it up without hesitation.

I was still staring at the smear on the floor. The old slogan, "Reach out and touch someone," came to mind, only this time with a whole new meaning, cause there ain't no one important enough to put that phone anywhere near any part of my body. I guess this stuff doesn't only happen in the movies.

Just then, Jose the "boofer," (prison slang for hiding things in your anal cavity) lets out a quick whistle to get my attention. I glance over to see him squatting, per-

Wrong!

fecting his disappearing hand trick again.

"Pass this to other Jose," he whispers, barely moving his lips, staring straight ahead.

"Are you crazy?" I was still thinking AT&T, wondering what in the world would possess a man—

Just then, quick as a cat, Jose threw something else behind me. This time it landed with a slight thud. So, again, a quick peek and…well, there are no words, Dad.

The cell phone wall charger, boxed and ready for prison.

Yes! The box.

Before I could make sense of any of this, the slot opened and the CO yells, "What in the **** is going on in here!?"

Dad, I had only two thoughts: 1) *Square things can come out of a round hole?* and 2) *I'm not gonna make it in prison.*

Can you please come back, Dad???

Love you,
J

P.S. Since you and I are always up for clichés, here's one for you: "Whatever doesn't kill me only makes me suffer and wish I were dead."

Doctor Knows Best

Dear Dad,

Society is much more tolerant of medicine than drugs. "Drugs" is what you buy from a guy named "T-Bone Walker" on any urban block and "medicine" comes in a plastic bottle personalized with your very own name. Now Dad, this form of intake is always acceptable, right? After all, "Dr. Harvard" sold it to you in a plastic bottle with directions and your name on it. Get my drift? I am guilty of abusing both medicine and drugs, but Dr. Harvard's is the only one that almost took my life.

Dad, Ambien is a miracle sleeping drug and for me, a year's supply disappeared in about a month. I could abuse this medicine right in front of my loved ones, and like a dying king, they had no more authority. Coaches, Mom, and my friends weren't as intelligent as Dr. Harvard so they didn't bother to tell me I was out of control.

I couldn't travel with T-Bone's medicine on airplane or in car consoles, or unwrap a foil package of it to soothe my nerves after a worrisome phone call. Especially not in front of a bunch of people. But Jayson has so much money that he must have the best doctors who give the best medicine and advice. Wrong!

Before I came to prison, I was involved in a highly publicized alleged drug overdose. The news reported that I was dead or on my way to being dead because I overdosed on prescription Ambien. I was in a hotel room, knocked out on Ambien, and woke up to flashlights, shouting, and police officers in full-combat SWAT gear breaking down my door. At first, I thought I was being robbed, figuring someone must have known about the Rolex watches and checks I put in the safe earlier. I jumped up, confused and ready to defend myself, and was ordered to freeze or get tasered. I chose the electricity.

I always have to stop and laugh when I think about my first thought when I saw the police officer begging me not to make him shoot me with his taser. I was thinking, *Hey! I had that gun when I dressed up for Halloween when I was eight.* I was Captain Kirk from the Starship Enterprise. When the taser hit my back, I instantly knew I had never possessed such a weapon.

My arms bounced together, along with my legs, butt cheeks, and private parts. No Sir, I never possessed such a weapon! I began negotiating. Anything they wanted was theirs. *Just please, Officer, don't electrocute me again!*

I remember lying so still on my hospital bed on the psychiatric ward at Bellevue Hospital, too afraid to move or touch the remote control for fear of being electrocuted. I threw my back out lying there in one position for 13 hours straight! Thank you Jesus for letting me laugh about this now.

The police didn't happen upon my hotel room that night by chance. They were called there after I fell asleep while talking to a friend on the phone about some serious issues. Nevertheless, I was a drug abuser. I would drink heavily, get more depressed, and then over-medicate myself with prescription drugs, hoping to somehow wake up from this nightmare that was my life. But no, I just woke up to a different nightmare and more insanity.

T-Bone Walker and Dr. Harvard should have never been involved with me. I'm smart enough to have diagnosed myself. Now that I know what's wrong, the rest is easy. Run—don't walk—run to Jesus. Ask him for peace and joy. And trust Him. Don't put a time limit on things. Once you pray, it's done.

I have to be honest. Because I was so afraid of going to prison, I traded Jesus in, fired Dr. Harvard, and then manipulated "Dr. Yale" for another prescription. This prescription led to my first DWI and the only prescription I ever needed. *Jesus.*

1 Peter 5:7 says I can cast all my anxiety on my Father God and He will give me peace. Trust me. It's no cliché. It's that simple. *"The peace of God, which surpasses all understanding."* No drug on this planet is capable of mimicking this peace.

It took a prison sentence to isolate me with God. Why should I worry? As long as I believe that Jesus died for my sins and I've repented and accepted Him as my Savior, I have nothing to fear. I've found peace in prison, of all places. Now, instead of taking medicine to go to sleep for days I can't wait for 5 a.m. because therein lies my joy. No more aluminum foil or plastic bottles. Dosage now reads: *Take Jesus as much as possible.*

Love and miss you, Dad,
J

P.S. He who never recognizes his failures is he who never grows out of his failures.
~ Barry Rand, President of AARP

The World's Tallest Chemist

Dear Daddy,

They transferred me to St. Vincent's Psychiatric Ward after my taser incident at the hotel and alleged sleeping pill overdose. The media reported it as an attempted suicide. I remember the doctor saying that they pumped my stomach and took my blood, but found nothing to indicate it was a suicide attempt. I didn't tell the doctor at the time why I wasn't trying to kill myself. I had a couple reasons why I wouldn't. Suicide is eternal damnation and I was too much of a coward. No noble clichés like, "I didn't try to kill myself because of my mom or my kids." I wish I could have been that unselfish. Suicide? No. Assisted suicide? Maybe.

Like in 1 Kings 19:3, Elijah actually wished for death, too, but he prayed that his death would be at the Lord's hand. I acted irresponsibly and loose at best. Dying wouldn't have been an intentional act on my part because that would have meant that they had won. Just like Elijah didn't want Jezebel to take his life, I felt the same way.

A high-ranking police official explained to me that they would have to arrest me or turn me over to the supervision of the psychiatric ward. As he was telling me, I saw Tanya Young dressed well enough to take to Chinatown. I instantly thought to myself, *No way on God's green earth this woman could put on that much make-up and her Sunday best and still rush to my bedside.* My bedside for artificial reasons, yes. And a press conference, definitely.

So as she stood there looking concerned the police officer and doctor asked me if I knew who this person was.

"Yes," I answered. "She's one of the reasons I'm in here. That's my ex-wife." (Legally, not yet. The divorce she filed for is still not final.)

"Do you wish to talk to her?" The doctor asked.

"No, let her go and do her press conference." I responded. I knew that two people with deep issues toward each other—and just issues period—can't sharpen each other. Water and oil. Enough said! I won't talk anymore about Ms. Tanya Young because I hope we have both moved on in the peace and joy of God's love.

Twenty-three hours after I arrived at the hospital, I got up and showered so I could check out, like this was just another night I had to sleep off in a less-than-average motel room with a whole lot of room service, no food, but a lot of attention. I already knew this was nothing more than a bad mixture of sleeping pills and Vodka, further complicated by a new ingredient, something prescribed to one of my friends for balance. My experiment as the "World's Tallest Chemist" failed.

As I headed toward the exit door, a bunch of people suddenly rushed over to re-route me straight into a private room filled with white coats and concerned faces, about 10 of them, if I recall. Their first question to me was, "Do you hear voices?"

The World's Tallest Chemist

Dad, their serious looks were too heavy for me so I broke the ice with my bar skit. I delivered my first line in a loud and jovial voice. "What's this!? Last call for alcohol!? Ugga Bugga, Ugga Bugga!" I started moving around the crowd of white coats, jumping and dancing while singing, "Ugga Bugga, Ugga Bugga!" It was always a hoot in front of my fraternity buddies. But this wasn't my fraternity.

Not accustomed to a comedy skit going wrong and after trying to be a seasoned comic and continue, I just stopped. I looked around the room for a friendly face. Even the African American lady knew the Ugga Bugga skit just got me committed.

So, like a comic who didn't really care that his skit went terribly wrong because he was paid in advance, I shrugged and headed for the exit. I could feel that I was being watched but not followed. *Weird*, I thought, *but what the heck.* I reached up to turn the doorknob, and noticed a sign saying that I needed to be buzzed out, similar to a small jewelry store that had been robbed one too many times. The president of the hospital came down and explained to me that I should grab a Snickers candy bar because I was going to be there for a while. Dad, he wasn't lying! I spent the next seven days in this psychiatric ward. I think it's fair to say Jesus tried *everything* to get my attention. A psychiatric ward! Now that's classic!

Mark Twain said, "When we remember we are all mad, the mysteries disappear and life stands explained." We all have issues—we just have to find out what they are. Dad, you once told me that a person who is his own doctor has a fool for a patient.

While I'm dealing with my issues in isolation and when I'm released I will remember what you said about great services not being canceled by one act or one single error. Try our best is all we can do.

Love you,
Jayson

No Strings Attached

I often wonder while I'm sitting confined by blocks and steel, What is my best friend Joe doing? Is he on the golf course? Is he having dinner at Tavern on the Green? What in Sam Hill is my best friend doing? Is he making a toast with my other friends while having 2007 Pinot Noir from Oregon? Is he even thinking of me?

The answer is, *Yes, Jay, I'm thinking of you every second of the day.*

Is that you, Joe?

No, Son, it's God.

Of course it is. Who else wants to have a 100% relationship with me, with no strings attached? God, that's who! The First Commandment says you should not put anyone before Him. Great relationships must have priority in my life above everything else. Life without love is really worthless. Four of the Ten Commandments deal with our relationships with people. But all Ten Commandments are about relationships. So I guess I'm saying (before I have to stop writing and be counted by the corrections officer), I must remember to prioritize my relationships. Love God and then love people (family and friends). Love will last forever, along with faith and hope. I hope I'm not remembered by how many points I scored, or how many crimes I've committed, but how I treated people. That is the most enduring impact I can leave on earth.

Roots

Dear Daddy,

Hopefully we are going outside to the Big Yard this morning for recreation. It will be the first time since the day before Christmas. The winter weather is still a major safety hazard because the inmates use the snow cover to hide weapons. Anyway, this will be a quick one.

I remember meeting Alex Haley on the streets of New York City about 10 years ago and explaining to him what kind of effect his historical, record-breaking mini series in 1977, *Roots,* had on me. I only had a couple of minutes and I don't think he really got what I was trying to say.

"Of course, Mr. Haley, I agree that slavery had terrible effects on all people—especially African Americans..."

But there was a deeper connection, one that was probably a little one-sided and selfish, looking back on it now. See, Daddy, I was trying to tell him how crazy you were for moving my white mom and me, your son, who was— heck, something like a High Yella, with an orange complexion, with blonde, John Travolta (Saturday Night Fever) type hair, to the poor, low-educated Deep South.

I was telling Mr. Haley in the middle of Times Square in December, "To heck with all the beatings Kunta Kinte took! Times that by five and you have one month of my school bus rides in Ritter, South Carolina!"

I will never forget the look on Mr. Alex Haley's face when he realized I was comparing slavery with my school bus experience. If I weren't 6'10 and one of the biggest entertainment slaves he had ever seen, he would have punched me right in the nose. I remember Mr. Haley treating me somewhat like a crazed, stalker-type fan.

"Okay. Whatever... Um...you said your name was Dr. J. or something? Well, I gotta go now."

But I insisted on walking with him in the direction he was going so I could finish my trilogy about the Deep South.

Riiiiiight. LOL. That lasted about two blocks when Mr. Haley hit his limit (justifiably so) and blew a fuse. No longer speed walking ahead of me, his pace came to a screeching halt.

He turned to face me, and said something like, "Don't think I'm too old to give you an old-man type whooping! Now get away from me!!!"

And right then, his writing skills came to fruition when he spewed out a talented rant, "Look, you giant Philistine-of-a-proud-petty-unjust-control-freak, vindictive fool-of-a-man, with a smell of Vodka and a twist of lime on his breath, get away from me before I blow this whistle I have in my pocket and you'll be in chains faster than Willie Lynch can write a letter to Jamesburg slave owners!"

And then he ran across Fifth Avenue, reminiscent of Kunta Kinte when he still had feet. Every time I tell you this story, Dad, you give me the same look Mr. Haley gave me, *Jayson, you giant idiot!!*

Daddy, I said all that to say this. You let me ride that southern school bus every day and endure those fights because (as you explain it), you couldn't hide me forever, and even a turtle who wants to move in a forward progression must stick his neck out to move.

So I kept moving, Daddy, and I kept riding that bus and enduring the daily assaults from the cowardly bullies until one day when (like Mr. Haley) I, too, had reached my limit. I got off the bus and marched right up to you and asked you why you married a white woman when you could have married a black woman just as easily. You popped me upside my head and picked me up off my feet to your level. Staring eye-to-eye, our noses practically touching, you sternly said, "Don't you ever say that again!! I picked your mama, but God painted her!" And even at eight years old, Daddy, that was funny. You lowered me to the ground with no more punishment and we laughed together (at Mom's expense, of course), and bonded for the first time. Then you became serious again and asked me where I learned that.

"On the school bus," I replied, without skipping a beat.

Well, I never rode that school bus again, and not because of the beatings by the cowardly bullies, but because you explained to me even way back then that 85% of what a kid learns and imitates comes from his peers on the way to school. Children gravitate toward whatever pleases the important people (the bullies) in their lives, right or wrong, out of their need for acceptance. My first lesson from you, Dad, was to be mindful of the company I keep.

We have a Bible study on our tier here in prison and 24 out of 38 inmates take time out to praise God in the middle of the day. I explain to them through God's Word that we must submit to God and surrender to become stronger. Dad, it's the most beautiful thing in the world (besides my daughters) when these prisoners stop what they are doing to give the Lord 10 minutes of their time in a place like this—where showing [what the devil considers] weakness can be dangerous. We study a different character in the Bible, pray, then drop to the ground and do 50 push-ups. The body, mind, and spirit are receiving Jesus. Every once in a while we will get a prisoner who just wants to sit on his pity pot, and I assure them, "It's all right. Just remember to flush when you are done."

Daddy, I know you have your rounds to make in Heaven, and I'm sorry this letter went this long, but they canceled the Big Yard. Oh yeah, if you see Mr. Alex Haley up there, please explain to him that I'm not deranged and crazy.

What? Hold on, Dad, I can't hear you. What? He's not dead yet?

Wow. Maybe I am crazy. Just don't tell anyone, especially Mr. Haley.

Love you more this morning...more than ever.
Jayson

II.

If you could kick the person in the pants responsible for most of your trouble, you wouldn't sit for a month.
~Theodore Roosevelt

Problem Solving
Father of the Year
Fanatics
Will Power
Left Behind
Selfish Antenna
Molasses in Wintertime
Snitches Get Stitches
Show Me the Baby
Work the Land
Hand to the Plow
Double-Edged Sword
Open Your Jacket
Compassion
Funky Cold Medina
Mr. Deuce

Problem Solving

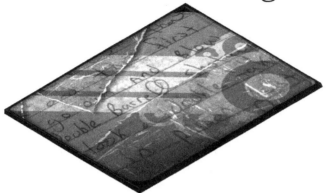

It's 9 a.m. on Thursday and time for my Problem Solving class with Mr. Lodderhoss. Mr. Lodderhoss is a 64-year-old white man with gray hair who everyone calls "shot out" because of his personality. That's prison slang for a person who has been locked up so long that he becomes, on his best day, two tacos short of a combo plate. Mr. Lodderhoss, standing in front of his classroom full of hardened criminals, begins with a typical icebreaker.

"WHAT THE HELL ARE YOU DOING? You are touching your face! Don't you know you were touching your face? Yes, well, you get one demerit anyway." After about 20 minutes of these anecdotes, he officially begins.

I always find it amusing how Mr. Lodderhoss can intimidate, or should I say hold captive, his audience of prisoners using the element-of-surprise technique. Before you know what hit you, he is on to the next topic. But this day was a little out of the ordinary.

Today Mr. L asked the class, "What's on your mind?"

You must understand that most people just take

this class so they can get an extra visit each month. First time offenders often take it to try to gain favor with the parole board. However, showing up is always more sufficient than class participation. And today, like every other day, nobody wanted to stay any longer than necessary. So why ask questions that might jeopardize our dismissal?

Not so fast, say it ain't so, a hand rises in the back.

I slide down in my chair, hoping not to be part of why this inmate is raising his hand. Maybe it's gonna be more of this, "Who was the f***ing hardest player you ever played against?" nonsense.

Not this time. Barry, a 64-year-old black man who resembles Morgan Freeman except for his bald head, has something on his mind. Barry doesn't notice our annoyed sighs and mean looks and Mr. L isn't paying attention to him either. So Barry clears his throat and then blurts out real loud, "I'm getting out next week." Then he tells us that the first thing he is going to do is go out and blow his wife's head off with a double-barreled shotgun. That's what he said, verbatim.

Now, I'd like to think I have a pretty good read on most of the people I meet. Here in prison I analyze inmates just to pass the time. I guess about their lives before prison. *Do they have a family? A disease? A career? Do they like hot sauce?* And it's not always complicated. Sometimes a simple word or phrase can accurately define a man. *The wheel is spinning but the hamster is dead.*

Analyzing people in prison is fun, and I like to think that I'm right on the money most of the time.

Except for Barry. I thought he was someone I might enjoy fishing with.

Okay, back to class.

So Barry had his outburst and out of the corner of my eye, I see that everyone's just carrying on like usual. Not one person, including the teacher, seemed

Problem Solving

concerned. So I start to relax. *Barry was probably just joking*, I tell myself. *Maybe this is how people joke in prison.*

Barry then calls out the name and address of this soon-to-be victim. *Becky from Camden.* "Yeah, that b**** broke the Golden Rule," he calmly added.

Mr. Lodderhoss says nothing. No one says anything. Then Mr. L picks up where he left off and continues his lecture for about 40 more minutes. He talks about primary energy and how it might be affecting Barry, and some other stuff I can't remember, and oh yeah—the basics on how to build a spaceship and go to Mars. *Is this for real? Somebody!?*

Barry begins to chuckle with a you-amuse-me grin on his face, then turns to Mr. Lodderhoss and says, "Mr. Whatever-Your-Name-Is, I'm really going to kill that b**** now."

Mr. Lodderhoss looks at his watch and says, "Barry, let's pick up on this next week."

Now, I see three immediate problems with, "Let's pick up on this next week." 1) At the very least, Barry should probably stay after class, a little one-on-one might be necessary here. 2) Barry leaves prison before the class meets again. 3) The police and Becky should probably be made aware of these small innuendos.

None of these things seems to be happening, so I walk over to address Barry about not killing his wife.

"I have a question fo—" I begin.

Barry interrupts, "Man, I've been meaning to talk to you, Jayson Williams."

Right away I'm thinking, *Okay, we're making progress and I'm gonna save a life.* I lean in real close. "Barry, what's on your mind?"

He's not saying a word, just staring at me. Then, as if he had not said anything alarming in class earlier, asks, "Jay, who was the f****** hardest player you have ever played against?"

I had no response for this 64-year-old violent fool. I walked back to my cell and laid on my cot to reevaluate things.

Father of the Year

Paul asked, "Who has known the mind of the Lord that He may instruct him?" I Cor. 2:16

It's 3:55 a.m. and I couldn't fall asleep here in Hotel DOC. So as a pre-Father's Day exercise, I thought I would stay up and observe my fellow inmates. Thirty-four out of 37 on the tier are fathers. That's about 90%, but that's 100% that won't make it home for Father's Day. My first thought is how sad this must be for these fathers and their families.

Then God spoke to my heart these words, "Be still and know that I am God." In other words, "I make no mistakes." God is not filling my mind with sorrow, but with knowledge about Him. A very high percentage of my fellow inmates are child molesters. Now, are their families or other families safer because they are here being rehabilitated? I can't question God on this issue. I can only say that I'm not up for "Father of the Year."

While some inmates here may have hurt children and need medical attention or therapy of some sort, I have my own issues. I am just selfish. Selfish enough to be reckless! Thank God my victim wasn't a father, but he was a son, and a brother and loved by so many more. Only one prayer can give me peace at this early hour.

Oh Lord and King: please expand my boundaries so I can impact the lives of many in the name of Glory! Please keep me from evil that I might cause no more pain. Amen!

Fanatics

In prison, friendship is the difference between doing time (which is okay) and letting time do you (which is not okay).

I have two friends in here. Matt is a professional soccer player. We enjoy Bible fellowship together and playing sports. I have another friend who is a former pro boxer. I only write this because Matt is truly a man of God. Johnny is still trying to figure his relationship with God after 52 years. Both guys have terrible tempers and big, fragile egos. So any sporting event where we compete against each other is to say the least, close to a fight breaking out. One and a half men of God can't agree to disagree.

"The same diamond looks different from different angles." A bad call on the handball court (a non-contact sport, let me remind you), can lead to a fight that can add more time to your sentence. How selfish is that? How do you explain that because your ego was bruised you won't be home for yet another Christmas? Two grown men of God, or again, one and a half, will argue everyday about the same thing.

My dad always told me a fanatic is someone who can't change his mind and won't change the subject. Neither one can win when they play each other because the devil has already declared game, set, match. Thank God I have friends like this so I can learn from their mistakes – because I can't live long enough to make them all myself. I will be home for Christmas!

Will Power

The hurt and pain I caused could have been avoided if I gave my relationship with God a fraction of what I devoted to vanity. You cannot fight vanity with will power. Yes, will power can produce short-term change, but it creates constant internal stress because you haven't actually dealt with the root cause. The change doesn't feel natural, so you eventually give up and revert back to your old patterns. I did countless times.

My fellow inmate Nick gave me an example about trying to go west in a speedboat that is programmed to go east on autopilot. I can turn the steering wheel and fight the autopilot, but it will eventually just tire me out. That is will power. It will work until I become exhausted. I must change the autopilot, my thinking, if the change is going to last. That's the long-term solution. No more vanity because that belongs to the devil, and it will get me every time.

I must continually remember what God said in Isaiah 46:9-10, *"I am God and there is no other, I am God and there is none like Me. I make known the end from the beginning, from ancient times, what is still to come. I say: My purpose will stand, and I will do all that I please!"*

Now does that sound like someone I can bargain with? Absolutely Not!

Foolish me! Forgive me, Lord.

Left Behind

It's 8:30 a.m. We have second recreational outside in the Big Yard. This is when 700 people who are deemed a menace to society all bring their opinions to one common ground, the Big Yard. There is hardly any place or any company where you may not gain knowledge, if you please. Almost everybody knows some ONE thing and is glad to talk about that ONE thing.

Thank God that He has blessed me with speed. This helps me get out of the conversational headlock. If the guy you are jogging with is a foolish man, then you just speed up your pace, and like a man who doesn't believe in God, he's left behind!

Selfish Antenna

I know why I'm in prison. It's because of my selfish ambitions. I am working hard to be inspected, then corrected, and hopefully respected. But believe me, breaking the habit of selfishness and vanity is a lot harder than breaking an addiction to any drug man can manufacture. That's because selfishness and vanity aren't manmade, but from a fallen angel.

For example, when people who I didn't spend much time with on the street ask to come visit me, my selfish antenna goes up and I ask what do they want to see, me or prison? It would make great conversation. "I went to prison today to visit my friend." Then continue with, "My friend is Jayson Williams." Wow, that's E.F. Hutton type of stuff right there!

Hey, they just might care for me, who knows? I've been wrong before. Heck, that's why I'm in here, right? I always make it all about me. And even when they are sincere, I can flip it. I prove what I want to prove, and the real difficulty is in knowing what I want to prove. Got that? I didn't think so. Only I would think so selfishly. I must open my mind because like a parachute, it only functions when it's open.

So what the heck, put my new friend on the visiting list!

Molasses in Wintertime

Today's Topic:

Everyone who hears these words of mine and puts them into practice is like a wise man who built his house on the rock.
~ God

They always seem to find me. I can be doing anything, anywhere, but don't want to be bothered just for a short period of time – not possible! I can pick up a Bible, I can look angry, I can even be sleeping, but they still find me.

I can't blame it on prison, because this happened even when I was on the other side of the wall. If I found myself in a conversation I had no interest in, I would just listen anyway. For this, I pleasantly blame God. He blessed me with charisma that draws crowds, regardless of what I'm doing. That's why I ran from God all these years. I wanted to gather people to do what I wanted to do, not necessarily what God wanted me to do.

After the accident, the media made me infamous. As sick as this next statement sounds, it's true. I was relieved. I thought I would have some peace, that maybe people would be scared of me.

Not!

You know what? I'm lying to myself. To think is to say no and everyone knows by now that I'm not going to say no. I'm gonna listen to all their so-called problems and then watch as my advice moves through their heads as slow as molasses in the wintertime. Thinking for others is exhausting. So is being yessed to death by inmates who go back to the same follies just as soon as I turn my back.

Thank you, God, for the blessing you bestowed upon me to draw crowds. And I also thank you for making me 6'10" and 250 lbs. so that these fools at least wait for me to turn my back.

Most people who ask advice of others have already resolved to act as it pleases them.
~ Knigge

Snitches Get Stitches

I'm reflecting on how to put what we learned during Bible study into practice. Turn the other cheek. Here in prison, this can be dangerous for your reputation. For example, if a "punk" inmate snitches on you for something he's doing too, inmates expect you to retaliate. If you don't, you are now viewed as a punk.

Now, let's watch how the devil premeditates prison problems. He builds up your reputation and ego until you become naïve and self-confident enough to foolishly let your guard down. Now I want to peel this inmate's skull for telling on me for something I shouldn't have been doing in the first place. Wow, I'm wrong twice.

So in Bible study, when I was relearning how to turn the other cheek, I didn't feel the presence of the devil. But as soon as I tried to practice what I learned, that's when the Father of all Lies got upset. So thanks be to God I had some scripture I could repeat to myself to keep myself from the temptation of violence. It went something like this: *God sets himself against the proud, but He shows favor to the humble. So humble yourself, Jayson, before God.*

So I untied my state-issued boots, which are great for kicking snitches, and laid down on my cot. I'm putting my head in Jesus' bosom tonight, and asking Him to keep me from putting these state-issued boots in someone's chest tomorrow.

Show Me the Baby!

Three comedians are shooting the breeze at the back of a nightclub after a late gig. They've heard one another's material so much that they've reached the point where they don't even need to say the jokes anymore to amuse each other—they just refer to each joke by number.

"Number 37!" cracks the first comic, and the others break up laughing.

"Number 53!" says the second guy, and they howl.

Finally, it's the 3rd comic's turn.

"44!" he says. He gets no laughter, not even a chuckle.

"What!?" He looks disappointed and asks, "Isn't 44 funny?"

"Sure, it's usually hilarious," they answer, "but the way you tell it..."

In prison I expect a whole lot more from a circuit of preachers that visit once a week. I'm locked in a room with people who repeat the same negative selfish ambitions 24 hours a day, all week long. So I put all my eggs in one basket: Sunday's service. Each week I go to prison church hoping for a "word" to warm my spirit. But for some reason, I'm just not getting the messages these preachers are attempting to deliver. I don't know if the preachers are just ill prepared or if they were never trained on how to tell a parable like Jesus. Jesus had to be a great storyteller to keep the attention of thousands who were sitting on the ground, in the sun, and with no megaphone. These preachers are civilians who do noble things by giving their time and they come from a long ways away, but don't tell me about the pain, *show me the baby*!

The other problem is that most of the inmates here are on milk, not meat, in the Bible. In other words, this is new to them. Either way, the devil's tricks haven't changed much. In years past, he always tried to attack me right after the church service because I was so on fire for the Lord. You can't leave church saying, "I understand a little bit of the message." That's like saying, "I'm a little pregnant." We must become "doers of the Word," and actually do what the Bible says. Satan doesn't mind us going to church and receiving the message as long as we don't do anything with what we learn when we leave.

I know beggars can't be choosers. I even find myself silently rooting them on, *Come on, Preacher, give it some gas, come on, you can do it!* But it's pretty bad when I have to "sell" prison church to caged men. Inmates flat-out refuse to go or they might go once and never again. These are grown men, locked up in cages 24/7, and they are choosing their cell!

David Letterman has always been very clear about the type of guests he likes on his show, "I don't care who you are, I don't care what you do. If you have four funny stories, you can be a guest on this show. That's what we're looking for."

But we aren't even that picky and you don't even need four stories, or even two.

Heck, I'll take one, and it doesn't even have to be

that funny, so long as you're prepared. But it's a shame when an inmate would rather spend an hour in a cage than an hour in church—in PRISON, of all places.

But regardless of my feelings, it is my responsibility to protect the unity of our prison church so I'm going to try not to harp on the shortcomings.

"Let us concentrate on the things which make for harmony and the growth of our fellowship together." (Romans 14:19)

Work the Land

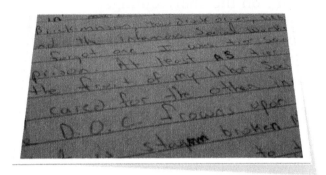

Yesterday I quit my job as a social worker's aide here at the prison. I didn't see any chance of advancement to—let's see—a civilian. This job was humility at its best and that's why I stuck with it for 33 days. You had to be searched everyday. You had to ask the secretary for the code to use the copy machine. Best of all, my personal favorite (like a scene from Cool Hand Luke —"Bathroom break over here, Boss?")—I had to ask to go to the bathroom.

They say we will have eight different professions in our lives. Well, let's see: truck driver, brick mason, tow truck driver, NBA player, pig farmer, gas station attendant, and now the infamous social worker's aide. Oh yeah, I forgot one...I was a "tier sanitation" worker here at the prison. At least as tier sanitation, I could see the fruit of my labor.

As a social worker's aide, I really cared for the other inmates' well being. The DOC frowns upon this. "If it's broken, let it stay broken." Not my motto at all. If it's broken I am going to try to fix it. But people in that office have become institutionalized and they go home

Work The Land

to their families every night. Their job has become routine, not commitment.

People at the DOC think they have all the answers. Inmates don't care what you know until they know that you care. My dad always told me, "Farmers work the land not to get the land, but to develop what they already have." We must learn to work together, inmate and civilian. No great work was ever done by just one person. "Many people are needed to fulfill a vision." How do I know when I'm serving God? The telltale sign will be enthusiasm. Well, I guess I'm on to job #8.

Hand to the Plow

It is always curious to me what we will do to escape thinking. My dad would always tell me that there is no bore we dread more than being left alone with our minds. But when you are a prisoner in a cell you have very few choices. I don't know if society was smart enough to factor that into the equation, but you need to ponder, not worry.

Meditate on God. Heck, if you already know how to worry, you know how to meditate. Don't dwell on all your mistakes in the past because the Bible even says in Matthew, "*Any man who puts his hand on the plow (for God) and looks back is not fit for the Kingdom of God.*" So we must recognize our mistakes and why we made them, then repent and pray. The rest is God's work. He doesn't need any help, trust me. God told me.

Double - Edged Sword

When I first arrived in prison I thought 75% of the people I met didn't belong behind bars. Now, after spending 24 hours a day with the same 75%, only one thought comes to mind: *Thank God we have penitentiaries.*

This morning was like no other morning I've experienced since I've been locked up. It was very active and most of the unit was up and about. This is because we are going to have an open bed.

The most consistent inmate I've met is leaving today. He's a young Muslim brother named Ali. He has finished paying his debt to society. If this man was my brother, I would be proud. Even though he is only 26 years old, he is very experienced with the criminal system. I like to be a clown, and he likes to laugh; thus, we had our own circus.

Sometimes all you need is an infectious laugh and to be consistent and people will go out of their way to be around you. Chris Rock told me that's why Adam Sandler gave him so many parts in his movies, for those two exact reasons. "Cause I can't act for beans, people just want to be around me," he explained.

And that might be exactly what brings my friend

back to prison. Ali will draw a crowd when he gets back home, but will it be the same crowd that got him here in the first place?

I prayed a special prayer for his success and wisdom on the other side of the wall, and reminded him that "character development always involves a choice, and temptation provides that opportunity."

A Salaam A'alaykum. (Peace be with you,) my Brotha!

Open Your Jacket

Sex charges are the most common amongst the prisoners here. If you are here at Mid-State Correctional Facility, it is most likely because you can't go anywhere else without being in harm's way. When I first walked into this place, I saw a person who had worked for me for 20 years. I didn't even know he was incarcerated and right away I wondered what he was in here for. But I took the Bill Clinton "don't ask, don't tell" approach, since prison is the biggest gossip house in the world due to so much idle time.

A high-ranking gang member approached me cautiously, using a pleasant tone, because that's the only way I would allow one of these community destroyers to talk to me. "Jay! Man, you have to watch the company you keep. That man is in here for raping his 11-year-old daughter."

Now, you don't even have to be a father to get upset over this. But now what? Do I treat him differently after this? Not just this guy, but at least 70% of the others here in Sodom and Gomorrah? There are 600 inmates who want to know me, but only one has told me his crime. And it was what we call "one of *those* crimes." In other words, he slept with a child.

On the one hand, I do treat sex offenders and pedophiles differently because I'm very cautious with my children's photos and addresses around these mentally ill people, as the Warden advised me to be. I also feel deeply for their victims, so much so that it is difficult to interact with them for any length of time beyond the "prison usual." Now, I hope they know they will be prosecuted and judged again someday by Someone much higher than any authority or peer here on earth. So maybe it's time to take off the mask and get some help. We are only as sick as our secrets.

Compassion

When he saw him, he had compassion. Luke 10:33

In prison people are always begging for something. Today I woke up for prayer at 3:50 a.m. Another prisoner saw this and took the opportunity to interrupt me and ask for toothpaste. Then he left without saying thank you.

Now, I'd had enough so I stormed into the bathroom to tell him he can't borrow anything from me ever again, but before I could get a word out he said, "Jayson, God sent you to this prison because you take care of everyone. I thank you, man."

I was surprised and thankful.

So just as I was patting myself on the back for not letting loose on him, he came back in and like he'd never seen me before and said, "Jay, can I borrow some deodorant?"

Only to me, and only in prison.

Do I have compassion for others?

Funky Cold Medina

When living among the backwash of society, the most confrontational bunch of misfits, you quickly learn that everyone is a jailhouse lawyer. They are the know-it-alls of the world. They know everything except how to stay out of prison.

Matt, Karroway, and I had a fellowship study this morning that quickly took on the tone of, "You are on milk in the Bible, and I'm on meat, Fool!"

Karroway insisted that God never said David was a man after His own heart. So the fellowship went in a different direction, the direction of *I know more scriptures than you*.

Then Karroway spewed out, with a serious face, "God also said, 'Peter Piper picked peppers' and 'I rock rhymes—' oh no, wait a minute, that was Run DMC." Funny, but sad, because the Bible was not given to increase our knowledge, but to change our lives.

So on that "Funky Cold Medina," I'm *Audi 5000*!

Mr. Deuce

I am a morning person. I absolutely love getting a jump-start on the rest of the world, and when I'm up and nobody else is, I feel that I'm outworking them. Now, what I must learn about prison is that I'm not waking up with my family in a Godly environment. I'm waking up with unpredictable people who I don't know.

On this particular morning, while I'm reading my Bible, I glance up and see an inmate named Mr. Deuce.

"Good morning!" I say.

Mr. Deuce shoots me a look of sheer surprise. "What the hell did you say?"

"Good morning," I say again.

Now Mr. Deuce's startled look goes right to evil and aggression. "When we get in the yard, I'm gonna kick your face in!"

Now I realize I'm not among family.

But never one to turn down a physical challenge, I say, "You gotta deal." Then I get dressed, tighten up my boots, and I'm off to follow my challenger to the yard.

I approach Mr. Deuce in the yard, who now has a look of submission.

"Mr. Williams, I've been in prison for 40 years and no one has ever said 'good morning' to me. Please accept my apology."

"No problem," I say.

Then, as we walk the track, he says, "You know, I'm a hermaphrodite."

Now I had a puzzled look.

"You *do* know what that is, don't you?"

"Of course," I lied. I'm thinking he's some kind of human reptile.

I guess after 40 years in prison he knew he was going to have to clarify.

"I have both organs," he explains.

"Me too," I reply. I'm thinking kidneys, but I've never been called a whatever–o–dite—

Then it hit me.

Holy Moley!! Both *those* organs!

He swore me to secrecy, which was easily obliged. Who in Sam Hill will believe that a man can have both what a mommy and a daddy have?! Mr. Deuce then went on his/her way leaving me dumbfounded.

Two months went by and I picked up a 10-day-old paper and an article caught my eye. Mr. Deuce, now MISS Deuce, as the article described her, picked up a man in a bar who had a knife, and had no idea what a hermaphrodite was either. Well, let me just say that Mr. Deuce is now *Miss* Deuce—-ALL THE TIME!

III.

May our Lord's sweet hand square us and hammer us, and strike off all kinds of pride, self-love, world-worship, and infidelity, so that He can make us stones and pillars in His Father's house.

~ Samuel Rutherford

Let's Blame the Athletes
Mr. Creative
Happy Birthday!
Cot in My Penthouse
Blvd. of Broken Dreams
Second Fiddle
Empty Seat
Purpose
House of Order
I Can Handle It
Sheep & Wolves
Rollies for Hep C
Man Amongst Boys
Fall Back
Isolation
Yes & No
Saggers
Mid-State Radio
Be Still

Let's Blame the Athletes!

There is no merit where there is no trial; and till experience stamps the mark of strength, cowards may pass for heroes and faith for falsehood. ~ Aaron Hill

I remember playing with Charles Barkley when he made a commercial for Nike and said, "I'm not a role model." I remember the outrage it caused; sports writers even used the word "blasphemy." Wow, is Charles God or a sacred entity? No, he's not.

Parental groups started picketing our arenas and practice facilities. Mothers, not fathers, screaming, "To whom much is given, much is required!" Well, not exactly because most of them didn't know any biblical scriptures anyway, if you know what I mean. But the message was the same.

Society is always trying to blame others for their failures. "If my son didn't watch your actions on and off the court he wouldn't have dropped out of Sunday school."

Unbelievable. The recipe for perpetual ignorance is this: Be satisfied with YOUR opinions and content with YOUR knowledge. Look, Ms. Picketer, what we do after the game is the same thing you do after a hard day in your office—have a beer or two. Why can't we drink and you can? Why are we supposed to be in charge of Lil Bobby? Heck, I've never even met your son! You are responsible for your own little litter.

When the Mrs. and Mr. Perfects of the world are driving through a ghetto and see all these young kids on drugs, they say, "That's really a shame" and they keep driving. When little Mrs. and Mr. Perfect get home and find Lil Bobby smoking a crack pipe, the first thing they scream is, "Oh my! It's an epidemic!" (Translation: all the little Mr. and Mrs. Perfect families are doing it now.)

Instead of pointing fingers from your little mansions in the suburbs and picketing everyone you think should be raising your own kids, why don't you sneak on over to that familiar medicine cabinet, take a prescribed drug, and calm down. Don't judge people, you hypocrite! Read Matt 7:3: *"And why do you look at the speck in your brother's eye, but do not consider the plank in your own eye?"* So before you go and blame someone else for failing in your duties, well heck, I don't want to sound redundant.

Oh yeah, and why did I say only mothers were outside the arena picketing and not fathers? That's because the fathers were inside the arena having a beer or two, in my office, while I'm at work. Now do you understand? Probably not. I will end with a quote that one of my college professors at St. John's University always had posted right above his desk. It stuck with me over the years. *The chief aim of wisdom is to enable one to bear with the stupidity of the ignorant.*

Mr. Creative

I read a quote by Donald Trump that was taped up on our front wall by a new inmate who was trying to inspire the locals. "Creative people rarely need to be motivated —they have their own inner drive that refuses to be bored. They refuse to be complacent. They live on the edge, which is precisely what is needed to be successful and remain successful." Now, this inmate has never been locked up before, but will soon discover that in prison, there is no shortage of creativity.

Prison contains some of the most creative people on the planet and the most complacent, also. They are creative enough to rob, steal, murder, and rape our grandmothers and children. Any crime that is premeditated is 1) creative and 2) evil. Some inmates believe that being creative enough to trick a teenage girl or an elderly person makes them smart. No, this makes them EVIL.

Most inmates are hypercritical of other inmates so they can take the focus off of themselves or fly under the radar, so to speak. They have no problem showing you their paperwork, but this is when the creative-manipulative part of their brain kicks in. See, charges are so broad and generic that a rape can look like an assault on paper. The inmate knows this.

Some creative inmates complain that they don't belong in prison. I always think to myself, *Then why didn't you go to court and fight it out in front of a jury of your peers? Why would you now all of a sudden become complacent, Mr. Creative?*

I know why! Discovery!! Because if the police get creative and really check out who you really are—*Oh!* Now you *do* belong right here in prison.

So, now here you are in prison hiding from your true skeletons, and you've become more complacent than ever. Are you suddenly too complacent and selfish to get creative? Creative enough to find a way out to see those who love you? Creative enough to trick the old, but just coward enough to stay right here instead of facing the music out there?

Trust me, if you really thought your sentence was unfair in the whole basketful of your sins you've been caught (and not caught) doing, you would be writing letters to administration, lawyers, judges, etc. Now, if you've had a "come to Jesus" meeting with yourself, then let's talk. But until you repent, I'm now becoming creative also—trying to create an excuse to get you out of my face!

Happy Birthday!

Today's my Daddy's birthday. He is now serving the Lord. All day I went through stories about my dad. I wanted to write just how I felt about him and best describe his love for me. I asked God to show me how much He let my dad love me. Then almost instantaneously, this story was left to me by another inmate.

There was a blind girl who hated herself because she was blind. She hated everyone, except her loving boyfriend. He was always there for her. She told her boyfriend, "If I could only see the world, I would marry you."

One day, someone donated a pair of eyes to her. When the bandages came off, she was able to see everything, including her boyfriend.

He asked her, "Now that you can see the world, will you marry me?" The girl looked at her boyfriend and saw that he was blind. The sight of his closed eyelids shocked her. She hadn't expected that. The thought of looking at them the rest of her life led her to refuse to marry him.

Her boyfriend left in tears and days later wrote a note to her saying, "Take good care of your eyes, my dear, for before they were yours, they were mine."

This is how the human brain often works when our status changes. Only very few, like my daddy, remember what life was like before and who was always by their side in the most painful situations.

Happy Birthday, Daddy!
I love you,
Jayson

Cot in My Penthouse

Out in Jersey, Jayson and his dad are building a new foundation for an extended family.

Dear Daddy,

When I was little, I wanted as much of your attention as I could possibly get. I know you used to listen to Mom and me read our prayers at night. I was always allowed one question after we finished our regular prayers, and you would always lower the volume of Phil Rizzuto and Bill White's commentary on the Yankees game so you could hear my nightly request.

"Mommy," I said, vying for an Oscar, "I pray that 9x3=29."

Mom looked up from praying, seeming confused. "Why would you pray for that, Jayson?"

"Because I put that answer down on my math test," I said, just loud enough so you were sure to hear in the other room. Dad, I knew the answer was 27 because you helped me memorize my 9's, but I really wanted you to come to my school. And like my daughters who now render me a puppet in their hands, I had you dancing to my strings, also.

Sure enough, the next day, right in the middle of morning announcements, "Jayson Williams, come to the principal's office! Your father is here." I loved it when the principal would call my name over the loudspeaker. All the kids would whisper and tease me, saying "Oooohhhh! Oooh!! Jayson, you gonna get it! You're in trouble now!"

"My daddy loves me," I would brag, as I walked around school with my Leon Spinks tooth count and little chicken chest puffed out. I was proud because you took off work to come to my school. I figured the other children were just jealous because you loved me more than their parents loved them. Their parents never came to check on them.

And things were always that way between us, Dad. Sometimes you would even follow me into the locker room after my basketball games—especially after I had a bad game.

"Noooo...No. You're coming home with me," you would say, as you marched me past the other players and straight to the parking lot. We would drive to my penthouse in the heart of the city and you would unapologetically remind me, "Well, someone has to pay for this monstrosity of a house we're building, Son!"

Dad, you didn't care who was going out to dinner or where, or which celebrity or player—you would just hold up one hand and say, "Please." And that one word was enough for me to know I was staying in with you and my brother, Victor. You slept right outside my bedroom door on that cot you bought for $42 from the Army-Navy Store in town. LOL. Dad, you were so heavy that it sank down to just above the floor. I was probably the only NBA player who wasn't allowed to go out with his friends and whose daddy slept outside his door every night for an entire NBA season. And you were probably the only daddy who bought a cot just to keep his son on the straight and narrow!

So thank you, Daddy, because I had the best season that year. I don't think I got more sleep, necessarily, because every time you moved or got up to go to the bathroom during the night, I jumped up from my sleep, scared half to death of the loud popping and creaking, thinking we were being shot at by the enemy.

Love and miss you,
Jayson

Boulevard of Broken Dreams

Dear Daddy,

Monday mornings to me are very important because I like to start the week off ahead of the curve, (but in jail with 37 other selfish people.)

Matt and I use the front table to study God's Word, pray, write, etc. Sydney, who is a friend of ours and helps us with cooking our food, wants this and *only this* table every Monday.

Before I arrived, Matt and Sydney locked horns a few times. This is totally a control thing for Sydney. He wants to sit in front at "his table" and yell at everyone and make turning in your sheets a Bar Mitzvah. Just because you have been doing something a long time doesn't make it right. I used to have a friend who would say, "I've been sniffing cocaine for 42 years and I'm not hooked."

I guess you could say why don't we just move to the back table? Well, the back is oozing with gloom. TV news on the highest volume, cigarette smoke everywhere, conversations and language that would make a sailor gag. The only thing I give any of these so-called soon-to-be-rehabilitated-for-society folk any credit for is waking up. But if they didn't wake up, they would starve.

So why would Sydney ask us to go study the Bible in Sodom and Gomorrah? I will tell you why. Because Jesus is working through Sydney's lazy behind. God doesn't go to Utah to save people, He goes to Las Vegas.

Daddy, we made our way to the back and before we even sat down, a Jewish inmate asked us if Abraham slept with his sister. Only he used more sailor-ish terms. After clarifying that, we simply "surrendered to God's will and continued to lead by example."

Heck, NO, Daddy! I left Sodom and Gomorrah to go back up front and find Sydney. Matt stayed behind and studied his Bible.

After explaining the situation to Sydney, he replied, "You don't have to go to the back, you just can't stay in the front." So I once again retreated, Daddy, because I was about to do an immoral thing for a moral reason.

God, I will go anywhere for You. Even to the back of the jail called, *The Boulevard of Broken Dreams.*

Love,
Jayson

P.S. *"No temptation has overtaken you that is not common to man. God is faithful, and he will not let you be tempted beyond your ability, but with the temptation he will also provide the way of escape, that you may be able to endure it." 1 Corinthians 10:13*

Second Fiddle

I have spent every single Father's Day with my father, right? Wrong. This is the first Father's Day that I have spent exclusively with my Father God. As far back as I can remember, it was always breakfast in bed with Daddy, then lunch at a restaurant, and so on. Today, June 20, 2010, is the first time I ever woke up knowing God is who I must think about every day as I have my first Father's Day in prison. But I still feel a little bit like a Benedict Arnold. That's how much I love my daddy. But even my dad knows he has to play second fiddle to God today.

This day, the third Sunday in June, has become so highly commercialized. It should be a day when we think not only about our earthly dads, but also our Father in Heaven. Without Him, none of us would exist. Colossians 1:16 says, *For everything, absolutely everything, above and below, visible and invisible...got started in Him and finds its purpose in Him.*

Now I am finally beginning to understand God's plan for my life. I trusted God, but I didn't understand so many things about how my life turned out. It took this environment for me to understand that God is a jealous God. Well, Lord, I shall "be still" and know that You are my Father. So Happy Father's Day! Also, Happy Father's Day to my daddy who is sitting at Your table on his first Father's Day in Heaven. Since you make no mistakes, You have my dad with You and me in here. I also have to say Happy Father's Day to my ex-wife because today, she is the father!

Empty Seat

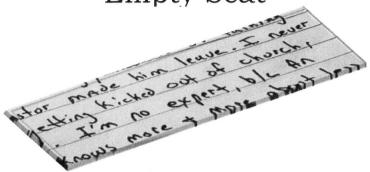

People are always blaming their circumstances for what they are. I don't believe in circumstances. My dad always told me to look for circumstances I want and if I don't find any, make some myself.

This is exactly what happened to one of my friends. Johnny Johnson was a boxing champion some 30 years ago. Now, at 52 years old, he can still throw a good punch. He is a very insecure, short-tempered man with a kind heart. But an argument needs no reason, neither does a friendship, especially if you want to fight the former champ.

Johnny believes in "sentence first and verdict afterwards." Not to go into details because who knows what will happen with this investigation and I'm easy to locate. I have learned if you don't say anything you won't be called on to repeat it. So that being said, let's just say Johnny and a gang member got into it over a seat in Mess Hall. The gang member ended up with a broken jaw and the champ is facing 4 more years on his sentence. Explain that selfishness to the wife and kids. Honey, kiss the kids and cancel Christmas. It all started going awry for Johnny five weeks ago when he was wrongly accused of talking in church. The pastor made him leave. I never heard of someone getting kicked out of church, especially in prison. I'm no expert because an expert is one who knows more and more about less and less; that's exactly how I feel; less and less.

To be continued...

Purpose

Even in prison, some days like today I can wake up on fire for God. So much so that I just want to hug Him, build Him a church, or do whatever I can do to make Him happy. I thought I would still be upset over Johnny Johnson getting kicked out of church by a preacher who was having an equally bad season. But I'm not! I now understand that the best use of life is to spend it for something that outlasts it. I'm going to step my game up for the Lord. I'm going to pray selfless prayers today like, "God bless me to do what You're blessing." Instead of, "God bless what I want to do."

Curtis Martin, a professional running back in the NFL, once explained purpose to me: *Wherever your skills and abilities meet the needs of the world, therein lies your purpose.* Well, today my purpose is to at least bring two people to Christ. I will no longer ignore this calling. If my neighbor were on fire, I would try to save him. Well, if my neighbor doesn't accept Christ ASAP, he will be on fire eternally!

But as soon as I start this mission, I expect the devil to throw all kinds of distractions at me. But I'm armed with scripture, *"Anyone who lets himself be distracted from the work I plan for him is not fit for the Kingdom of God."*

God, I want Your will, not mine. You have blessed me with the complete package, not for my use, but for Yours. I know You give me all I need from day to day. I must live for You and make the Kingdom of God my primary concern. Today I no longer feel that I'm on milk, but that I'm moving on to meat.

Amen.

House of Order

Sleep not when others speak, sit not when others stand, speak not when you should hold your peace, walk not when others stop.
~ George Washington, *Rules for Civility*

Every Sunday morning here in prison, Sydney, who is in charge of the TV, allows us to watch church TV. This is probably the only time that I voluntarily flex my muscle concerning preferences. I want the volume up as loud as it goes and insist that there are no distractions whatsoever. Now maybe I'm wrong to think everyone should watch the message from God in a house of order. I've been wrong before (or I wouldn't be writing this journal).

Okay, some things to keep in mind: (1) The volume should be at max, just like it always is for music videos. (2) Why in the heck can they cheer for any sporting event and not for Jesus? (3) Smokers come and smoke near the non-smoking Christians and then the non-smokers usually get up and leave. (4) Frankie or Francesca, as he femininely likes to be called, makes a big to-do-about-nothing scene to the administration, complaining that other inmates don't want him in church. They don't want him in church for the same reason I don't want him watching TV with us...he doesn't freaking shut up!

(5) Pat, the new guy who rapes young kids, sits with his back to the TV in an open defiance to us gathering around and repenting of our sins.

Okay, #5 is still breathing only because God is on TV and Mom used to say that God sees everything. When you are watching Him through the TV, He is watching you the same way through the TV. That was the sole reason I never watched pornography on TV.

I Can Handle It

The Monday that Johnny got excommunicated from the congregation and the jailhouse church, I didn't attend. I thought that the preacher was talking down on the inmates when he should have been encouraging us. I truly thought Johnny was trying to reveal his demons to a support group of Christians. We should have been preaching, "Don't repress it, confess it! Don't conceal it, reveal it!" Revealing your feelings is the beginning of healing. Right?

Wrong!

Johnny came to church for the right reason. The Reverend should have told all of us egotistic, selfish, sadistic, men of God this: The reason we hide our faults is pride! We want others to think we have everything under control. The truth is, whatever you can't talk about is already out of control in your life. If you could handle it on your own, you would have already done so. Some problems are too engrained, too habitual. You need a church or accountability partner.

But the preacher just threw him out instead. Now the preacher is not a prophet. He could not see into the future, but he could have handled the present much better. So could Johnny. Both men thought they were righteous; Johnny about a lousy seat when there were 400 more empty ones, and the preacher who thought he was being distracted. Both men should have taken heed to this; do not do an immoral thing for moral reasons. I will miss Johnny. What a tragedy!

Sheep & Wolves

Paul said, *"When I was a child, I reasoned like a child. When I became a man, I put childish ways behind me."*

I'm so selfish still after four months in prison I can't even see that I'm doing the same extreme foolishness over and over – makes me self-righteous!

Whenever I judge another believer several things happen. I lose fellowship with God. I expose my own pride and insecurity. I also set myself up to be judged by God. I know a critical spirit is a costly vice. Anyway, it's the devil's job to blame, complain, and criticize members of God's family. See, I'm using words like "believer" and "members of God's family." The people who I'm talking about, I'm not sure they are the former or the latter. Just because you go to church you are a Christian? Not true. The Bible says even the demons believe in God. I have never seen these people pray, read a Bible, or have a conversation about God since I've been here.

This is prison, and I'm still too nice to exclude people because they are non-believers. But I will no longer keep the company of blatant liars, cheaters, racists, rapists, and child molesters. I know I should use all my energy in getting along with everyone. I should encourage them, not drag them down by finding fault. But I will not keep the company of people who won't try to work on their sins and repent.

I'm tired of having the same conversations about these inmates. I feel like I'm spreading gossip. It is already sad that in God's flock, the greatest wounds usually come from other sheep, not wolves. Forgive me, O Lord, but I'm trying to get out of my selfish ways, and right now I must cut these people from my circle. If I stay away from them I won't talk or gossip about them. A fire goes out for lack of fuel, and tension disappears when gossip stops. The Bible calls Satan the Accuser of others, and I will never play for Satan's team. I *can* change the environment, but I will not try to change the man.

Rollies for Hep C?

Dear Daddy,

Jail fascinates people and they always wanna know, "What's the craziest thing you've seen in there?" That's easy. "Cigarettes!" I tell them. "You can lose your life in here over cigarettes!"

Now, I buy lots of cigarettes, but not to smoke. I have never smoked in my life and look forward to a time when the world will look back in amazement and disgust at a practice so unnatural and offensive, not to mention deadly. But everything (haircuts, laundry, etc.) is priced in cigarettes, which is our non-official prison currency. So I have seen more than my share of inmate fights in here over cigarettes, but that's not the dangerous part. It's the unsanitary conditions that will end up killing some of these inmates.

Dad, so many of these guys will just pick cigarette butts up off the floor and smoke them, not caring that the prisoners who dropped them consider prison a Ritz Carlton hotel. These smokers take this unprocessed tobacco—swept from the filthy floor— and roll it into cigarettes. They smoke these homemade rollies, then find themselves caught in a new routine of jamming

Rollies For Hep C?

toothbrushes down their throats and coughing up a lung for two to three minutes, at least twice a day.

At least when you ask someone for a drag of their cigarette, you can see the person handing you the filth. But when you sweep them up and recycle, it's a crapshoot with your life. Now, hold on Dad, if that didn't knock the halo off your head, there is something even more disgusting.

First off, you are not allowed to smoke indoors in NJDOC prisons. Now that we got the rules out of the way, let's talk about the environment. Daddy, some inmates really go green in here. They recycle twice. They pick up the butts off the floor, remove the rolling paper, and then dump the contents in a cup. That's once.

Now, they can't show smoke, because where there's smoke there's fire and you can go to "The Hole" (solitary confinement) for smoking indoors. So the inmates take the tobacco from the cup and chew it, then spit it on the floor, and then later after it dries, sweep it up and smoke it again. That's twice going green!

A few months later they are rewarded for being environmentally conscientious by receiving Hepatitis C. Yes, and they continue to use the same hardware that we use and better yet, they work in the kitchen.

Now you see why I'm back in shape, Dad? No mess food, less chance for Hepatitis C!

Love you, Daddy. (Sorry to ruin your five loaves and two fishes—or is it the other way around?)

Anyway, enjoy.
J

P.S. Life is hard; it's harder if you're stupid. ~ John Wayne

Man Amongst Boys

Dear Daddy,

I came in from lifting weights in the Big Yard, still on an adrenaline high, when I opened the Bible for my late morning Word.

I shouted, "I'm stronger than any four men put together in this prison!"

I didn't say it to put people down; I said it because I believe it to be a true blessing from God directly to me. For eight years I have carried the world on my shoulders, causing me to abuse prescription drugs, alcohol, and of course, my body. So after five months of training, my body is finally starting to run on all cylinders again. Whenever this happened in the past, I always stood back and marveled at how the Lord had created a man amongst boys. If this is—and it probably is—vanity, I shall repent right after I finish my journal.

So after I screamed my strength out and returned to my Bible (confident there were no serious competitors,) Brother Rice tapped me on the shoulder. Brother Rice is an evangelist and he is on fire for the Lord. "Turn to 1 Timothy 4:8," he says. And then he returns to his area and Bible.

1 Timothy 4:8 reads, *For bodily exercise profits little, but godliness is profitable for all things, having the promise of the life that now is and of which is to come.*

So I investigated a little further, and came upon 1 Corinthians 9:24-25. *And everyone who runs in a race all run, but ONE receives the prize. Run in such a way that you may obtain it. And everyone who competes for the prize is temperate in all things. Now they do it to obtain a perishable crown.*

I was surprised that the Bible even spoke of athletes, forgetting all about athletics starting in Athens. So I'm going to take this next part straight from my Bible.

In the Isthmian games, several athletes competed for one prize, but there could only be one winner. In contrast, the Christian life offers the opportunity for many people to be winners. The winner of the Isthmian games received a pine wreath crown. Those who faithfully complete the Christian life, on the other hand, will receive an imperishable crown.

Simply put, I know I'm physically secure, but am I spiritually secure?

Brother Rice put it in an even simpler form, "I'd rather be in a wheelchair and be spiritually strong, than physically strong and a spiritual invalid."

So, Daddy, I must get my endurance correct spiritually and then shout, "I am spiritually stronger than any four inmates put together in this prison!"

Say no more! Enough said!
Pray for me, Daddy.
Love you,
JW

Fall Back

I do not distinguish by the eye but by the mind, which is the proper judge of a man.
~ Seneca

One of the first inmates I saw upon arriving in prison was a Skinhead with "White Power" on the back of his neck. As I bent down to examine the rest of his ink, I saw the words, "I hate niggers." Ever since I was a young teenager, I have learned to quickly laugh at everything, for the fear of having to cry. I thought, Wow, one out of two isn't bad. I don't agree with "White Power" printed on his un-athletic body, but I do agree with "I hate niggers." Since my mother is white and my dad is black, I have seen niggers on both sides. A nigger to me is plain and simple an ignorant person, don't matter the race.

Somehow I knew Jesus was going to make our acquaintance. Just the day before in my journal I remember saying that we had some racist people in my circle, the worst kind of racist people—over 50 years old, pompous, and trying to hide their ignorance. My daddy

Fall Back

used to tell me he liked South Carolina because down there he knew who was racist. They would let you know! Up north, they just keep stabbing you in the back.

So knowing that I could not change these men around me, I made a decision to change my environment. Say *Hello* and *Goodbye*, because you can't avoid them entirely—we are all crabs in a basket in here.

But God wasn't going to make it that easy. If so, why start now?

So after the whole prison noticed that I've changed up my circle, here comes Miami Ink himself. A little harder to avoid because now he's so close to my bunk that I don't have to read the newspaper for evil, I just read my bunkie's back. As I sized him up, I noticed he walked with his head down and his shoulders slouched. I know that posture, I had it for the first 17 years of my life because of my biracial family. But I reminded myself not to rush to aid his low self-esteem. To be prepared for war is one of the most effectual means of preserving peace.

The inmates understand I won't tolerate prejudice of any kind on our tier. So before I went to address Matt about the Villain of the Day's tattoos, I noticed Matt was sitting in front of the TV with his shirt off, with a *Be Still and Know I'm God* tattoo on his back. As irony has it, the Villain was sitting right next to him with his swastika and "I Hate Everybody but Whites" in plain view. Two white men in their late twenties with two totally different outlooks on the world. So before I got up to address this man who has all this hate for Jews, niggers, and gays, I had to pray on it. I have often regretted my speech, but rarely my silence.

So after reassessing the situation, I see a young man who has made two mistakes. One, putting something on his body that is permanent and full of hate towards others. Two, coming to prison. (The latter being much more dangerous than the former.) So my final analysis for now was to "fall back." I have to defeat my temptation. I must *"run from anything that gives me evil thoughts, but stay close to anything that makes me want to do right."* (2 Timothy 2:22) For now this is time to be still and know He is God.

In closing, I think the Villain has experienced his fears, and put hate away. He is young and I'm personable, so I can work on the prevention, which is much less costly and far easier than trying to save the 50-something year old racist who now needs a cure. The difference between prison and freedom is that on the outside you might have to work with a racist. On the inside, you have to work *and* live with them for 24 hours, 7 days a week. This scenario is only new to me in prison, not on the other side of the wall.

So how will I go about trying to save the criminals from the Villain and vice-versa? I will tell him how good Jesus has been to me, and let Jesus take it from there!

Better to be ignorant of a situation than half know it.

Isolation

Dear Daddy,

In prison, isolation can metamorphosize many times. Because you are by yourself and in an unfamiliar and dangerous place, your senses heighten. If you are feeling uneasy about another prisoner you better become instinctive. For example, remember what an inmate's slippers and stride sound like so you will know if you are in danger when the lights go off. I mastered this skill at the young age of six when it was critical that I know who was coming up the stairs toward my bedroom. It was either tattletale Mom, who I could negotiate with to not tell you, or "The Enforcer" himself!

It's funny how generations can change within a family. When your two granddaughters are up to no good and they realize it's just me walking up the stairs, they breathe a sigh of relief. "Phew! That was close! It's just you, Daddy. We thought it was Mommy and we were scared!" Now I can only laugh and cherish these moments, and be glad the other inmates don't know I never wore the pants in the family.

Isolation can also be the worst possible counselor. It is sad not to be loved, but much sadder not to be able to love. While I'm isolated from civilization, I start to think about what that word means to me: truth, beauty, adventure, art, peace. I don't think the judge or anyone else ever anticipated I'd view isolation this way, but sometimes the byproduct is more valuable than the actual product.

Love,
J

P.S. Now, with God's help, I shall become myself. ~ Soren Kierkegaard

Yes & No

Dear God,

When I played in the NBA I was very outspoken, sometimes for the wrong reasons. I always knew You gave me the gift to change minds, and I tried to use it for good, but not always. Like how I "handled" my handlers. My father would always tell me, "You can't hang with the night owls and soar with the morning eagles," but I would manipulate my handlers to let me stay out an extra hour or so. Although I could persuade my handlers to say yes, I never learned how to say no, and this frustrated me to no end.

I am a person who has a hard time seeing someone not doing well, so my calendar was always full. I would say yes to every charity, every event, every foundation, and every so-called underdog. I would agree to charity events and then be upset two months later when I had to play six days a week in the NBA and still do all the charities. I remember being very difficult with my handlers, but when I arrived at the event and saw how many lives were affected, I always thanked them afterwards.

So many times I went out and did things I never should have done. The guilt and shame I felt afterward was so heavy that the day following a wild escapade of partying was often filled with more charity. I remember partying so hard one night that I woke up the next morning and sent 550 kids to a major university for free. It was my way of telling You to forget about the night before. But now I know better. My arms are too small to box with You.

Influence is powerful and I should use it for Your purpose, not mine. I mean, just imagine how much influence a guy like Lebron James can have on the world. Every step I take here in prison I'm asked the question "Where is Lebron James going?"

I want to say "To hell if he's not saved!" It seems that more people are concerned with where Lebron James is going than when Your Son is coming. I'm not being facetious when I say this.

If Lebron James would say "I'm going to Heaven when I die, and all kids should go to Sunday school every week," the prison system would go out of business.

In Great Britain, in 1955, they made children go to Sunday school and the crime rate dropped 65% over the next twelve years. I don't know if Lebron is even a Christian but if he is, he can change the world. He can get the world ready for the coming of Jesus, like John the Baptist. It's time that an alpha star speaks up for Jesus. Tiger Woods has the chance along with Michael Jordan. I'm not saying let the athletes raise your children, I'm saying let these billion-people megaphone stars just tell people about Jesus! Then, be still. You promised to do the rest!

Love,
Jayson

Saggers

Dear Daddy,

I do not watch American Idol but I did see the guy who sang the song, "Looking Like a Fool with Your Pants on the Ground." Whenever I spoke to young people, I would always start off by saying, "Please stand up. Now pull your pants up. First impressions mean a lot."

Now I'm in prison, and I've noticed that older and smaller inmates walk around with their pants on the ground. So I asked a man in the yard today (who looked as amused as I felt) how in the heck do their pants stay suspended below their buttocks?

"Jay," he began, "this trend started about 20 years ago down in Rahway prison. Younger and weaker inmates were repeatedly raped because they couldn't defend themselves against the larger, more seasoned criminals. After the weaker inmate was raped, he would go into a state of depression so the COs would have to take their belts and shoelaces so they wouldn't hang themselves to death. Without belts, their pants would naturally hang down off their butts. Experienced prisoners saw sagging pants as a calling sign and would know right away that the inmate was somebody's 'punk'."

Now don't ask me why people today on the other side of the wall proudly continue this trend. Maybe they have no self-esteem, or they're lazy, or they don't know the history I just explained. Because if they did, those unknowing punks would stop disrespecting my daughters and mom and pull their pants up off the ground. Sounds like another American Idol song, doesn't it?

So here comes the ripple effect. Because their pants are hanging off their butt, they have to walk with their feet pointed outward and moving side to side and pretty soon the Diddy Bop walk is in effect. Now since they have to take up the whole sidewalk because they are waddling side to side, they are late to work at the belt store. Any fool knows the shortest distance between a belt and its loop is a straight line!

Mid-State Radio

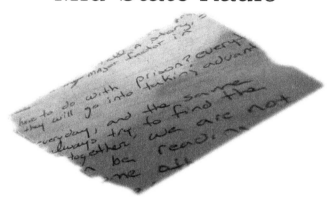

Bill Cosby used to tell me that people will always listen to what I have to say because I never let people figure me out. He said to never let anyone define you, and don't rush to define yourself. Mystery sells. (I added that last sentence myself.)

Eddie Murphy doesn't do commercials or interviews so that people will pay to see him in the theaters. My dad always controlled the room with his stories and infectious laugh. I worked my whole life on my so-called standup routine and I learned that if you can tell a story, I mean *a story*, you will always be a major factor in people's lives— hopefully for the better.

Now, what does all this have to do with prison? Everything! Soon as prison figures you out, they will go into taking-advantage mode. I have the same routine everyday and the same demeanor, which is consistently positive. I always try to find the humor in here in prison. If we are all laughing together we are not trying to hurt one another. Matt, a fellow inmate, and I can be reading our Bibles and, believe it or not, it will offend other prisoners. So this morning, Matt and I will interview the

Prince of Peace ourselves here on Mid-State Radio. Matt will play the interviewer and of course, I will play Jesus.

Matt: How are you, Jesus?

Jesus: Fine, thanks, and let me say it's great to be back.

Matt: Why, after all this time, have you come back?

Jesus: Mostly nostalgia.

Matt: Did you really raise Lazarus from the dead?

Jesus: First of all, he wasn't dead, he was hung-over. But I've told people that!

Matt: Well, what about the other apostles, say for instance, Thomas. Was he really a doubter?

Jesus: Believe me, this guy Thomas, you couldn't tell him nothin'! He was always asking me for ID. To this day he doesn't believe I am God.

It's 6 a.m. in prison with murderers, thieves and people who haven't said, "good morning" to anyone or better yet, smiled in 20 years. And if you've ever seen a seasoned prisoner's dental work, or lack thereof, you would know why they don't smile.

Anyway, the atheists and agnostics, and even a few male witches and the evangelist laugh hysterically. We accomplish two things with this because unlike Eddie Murphy, we can't pick and choose where we want to be seen.

(1) The whole prison is thinking of Jesus and the Bible says just tell them about me (Jesus) and I will do the rest.

(2) If they're laughing, we won't have to punch their lights out. For now anyway...LOL.

Trust me, Jesus has a sense of humor, He put me in here.

Be Still

"He leads me beside still waters." ~ Psalm 23

Today I read that sheep aren't great swimmers because once their wool gets waterlogged, they begin to sink under the added weight. Sheep know this and that's why most won't even try to swim in a current or drink from a moving stream. They feel most comfortable drinking from still waters.

Now, we are like sheep and we all have limitations. But God doesn't. God can do anything— even what seems impossible—but that doesn't mean He expects the same of us. He doesn't look down on us because we aren't always strong. He won't force us into a situation that is bound to fail, or insist that we do something we aren't prepared to do. He doesn't trick us or trap us. If He wants us to do something, He will provide what we need to get it done.

My trial lasted exactly eight years and one week. Every day and all day I had to—well, I should say *we had to* think about the trial. So every once in a while I would get a day off from the drama and would find a quiet lake to sit by. I would throw a fishing line with a bright red cork on the end way out into the lake and stare at the ripples that followed. Big lake, small cork, small splash, and the ripples kept going without any more help from me.

Sometimes I still want to control things, which here in prison is almost impossible. I get all uptight and high anxiety. Well, not anymore. I have made up my mind up for the final time to *"Be still and know that He is God."*

I'm so used to being the leader that it feels good to take the fallback order now. This doesn't mean I won't participate. It means I have prayed on it, and it has already been taken care of. Do with me what you want, Lord. I have made a pact with my soul not to worry any longer because You have my best interest at heart.

It's exactly how God blessed me in the NBA. He knew that with all the tragedies in our family, I would immediately jump off the handle. So He turned my game from offense to hustle. All I had to do every night was hustle as much as I could, and not worry too much about offense. Thus, no pressure. Hustle, just like praying, is a talent. Do all you can for the good of God and at the same time, "be still," knowing He would never harm us. The victory will be ours.

Just trust, believe, and obey. God must increase, but I must decrease.

IV.

We would rather be ruined than changed; we would rather die in our dread than climb the cross of the moment and let our illusions die.
~W.H. Auden

Good Morning
Yelling Shoes
Blowing Smoke
God's Giants
Bad Bored
Tears of a Clown
Lie Down
Both Sides
40 Men of Folly
Crabs in a Basket
Your Own
Come Back to Prison
Sorrow
More Grace
Back Pocket
Hirelings
More Coffee?
Chewed Out
Comfort Zone Bullies
Hit the Bricks

Good Morning

A.M.
5:15 - *eyes open*
5:20 - *pray*
5:25 - *brush teeth*
5:30 - *stretch & sit ups*
5:50 - *make bed*
6:00 – *pray again & start journal writing*
6:01 -*"Good morning" to all who pass by*
6:30 - *breakfast mess*
8:30 - *yard*

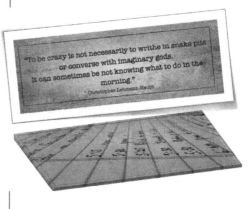

"To be crazy is not necessarily to writhe in snake pits or converse with imaginary gods. It can sometimes be not knowing what to do in the morning."
- Christopher Lehmann-Haupt

Every day in prison is like the movie *Groundhog Day*. My morning schedule hardly ever changes. Jesus wakes me up and says, "Jay, get up, man. We have to give our Father praise." Other inmates are awakened not by an alarm clock, but by one or more of their five senses— and sometimes a little more.

6:05 a.m. Inmate #26, a chain smoker, goes into the bathroom, coughs, then gags, then dry heaves until he vomits. Twenty percent of the inmates are awakened by their sense of hearing. It's loud and disgusting.

6:15 a.m. Beans are inexpensive and a cost-effective way to feed prisoners. But beans mixed with 40 men with low self-esteem and even less etiquette—the sense of smell wakes another 20% of the sleeping inmates. Oh yeah, speaking of beans, we have an 84-year-old inmate named "Beans" who killed his best friend for making a sexual pass at him one night.

6:22 a.m. This morning is already a little overcast so the tier is a lot darker than usual. As I pray on my cot, Brother Joe (we call him "Holy Joe" because he believes he is an anointed man of God) is across from me about 10 feet away, kneeling over his chair and praying. He does this every morning for about 20 minutes. Frankie, an openly gay man who looks like a British bulldog, screams out in his sleep at the top of his lungs, "Go Devils! Go Devils!" It's so loud he scares the devil out of Holy Joe, who plows over his chair at full speed and lands right on my cot.

Now Frankie always talks in his sleep, but this was ridiculous, and it woke up the remaining 59% of our tier of 40 inmates who all open their eyes to see a startled Holy Joe flopped across my cot. Not a good look for either one of us, the preacher lying across the pro basketball player in prison.

Then everybody does a double take as Beans, without missing a beat, jumps to his feet and points at us, shouting, "That's the same reason I had to kill my best friend!" Then he looks around for other inmates to cosign his plea...no takers, so the tier uniformly goes back to bed. Last time I looked back, I saw Holy Joe and Frankie about to fight; still not a good look for the preacher.

6:30 a.m. Breakfast mess call.

What a good morning!

Yelling Shoes

Dear Daddy,

You can't put the same shoe on every foot. This is my response to other inmates when they look down at my footwear situation. Now, I've never enjoyed running. It's tedious and I need action. But since I've been here at Mid-State, I run six miles per day, on average. That's about the same distance you'd run if you played in an NBA game for 48 minutes.

My running partner is a 6'3" 250 lb. ex-professional boxer who can be longwinded when it comes to his boxing days. Sometimes even a little punch drunkenness sets in and he tends to repeat himself. So being his junior by 10 years, when he starts with, "Let me tell you, when I fought Muhammed Ali..." I just speed up. Now he can no longer keep up the conversation at our new pace; thus, we both get in better shape in silence. Problem solved!

I run in the only footwear I own, a pair of construction boots with about 150 miles of running, basketball, and handball to their credit, and it shows. From the middle of my foot to the tip of my toes, the entire top half of the shoe has been totally ripped apart from the sole. When I go to put them on it looks like my shoes are yelling at me. I use elastic from my prison long johns to tie them up. Only problem is I have to pick my feet up an extra 16 inches or I will trip on my ugly face. I was 290 lbs when I got here and picking up my feet this high with every stride actually burns more calories; thus, I'm now 243 lbs. Problem solved!

I recently had to go to court in Burlington County. During this trip I encountered other inmates from other jails who thought they had it bad until they saw how the administration sent me there. A very irritated Muslim and about 20 of his associates thought this was racist. "How can a white man let you walk around like that, a black man of your stature?"

I calmly looked at Ali and said, "The administrator is not white, he's black." So I disarmed the angry inmate and neutralized the race card; thus, the life of the only white inmate in holding with us was spared. Problem solved!

My feet hurt so much from previous injuries and now from bad footwear. Every day I run barefoot on concrete, sharp rocks, and mud. Other inmates make jokes about my feet and humiliate me about my lack of adequate footwear and I just think about how my best friend Jesus must have felt when He was on the cross for something he had no control over. Thus, I love God for sending His only Son to die for my sins! Problem solved!

Love you,
J

P.S. Ali was so fired up about my situation he sent a letter to the administration. LOL.

```
                    NORTHERN STATE PRISON                                    105
                    P.O.BOX 2300
                    NEWARK,N.J.07114                    7/1/10


                    WARDEN:HUGHES
                    MID-STATE CORRECTIONAL FACILITY
                    P.O.BOX 866
                    WRIGHTSTOWN,N.J.08662


                                         RE:CLOTHING,ANDCOMMISSARY
                                            CLOTHING PERSONAL ITEMS.


            Dear Warden:

               This correspondence is on behalf of my brother JAYSON WILLIAMS
            whom is currently being housed in your facility.

            Today i personally witnessed him wearing boots that were the bott
            em of the soles of his boots were ripped off and he told me that
            he has had to wear them because he was not provided with anything
            else to wear.

            And that he has had them for five months,and he has been trying t
            o purchase clothing from the commissary for the past five months
            to no avail.

            Sir the man was looking like bozo the clown,and at risk to injure
            himself from wearing those boots.

            SO SIR WOULD YOU KINDLY LOOK INTO THIS MATTER.

            Thanking you in advance for your time and assistance in this dire
            matter.
                              CERTIFICATION IN LIEU OF OATH
             I certify that the foregoing statements made by me are true.I AM
            aware that if any of the foregoing statements made by me are will
            fully false,I am subject to punishment.

            CC:GOVERNOR
            COMMISSIONER                       YOURS IN HUMANITY
            S.I.D.
```

Blowing Smoke

In prison I awake every morning at 5:15 a.m. I first look around for my safety, and then pray. Then I take another look around for my safety, and then try to assess, did I have a dream last night or did I see what I thought I saw?

In prison, you can see some of the craziest stuff at night. Well, last night I thought I saw Frankie get the brakes beat off of him. Now Frankie is the master manipulator on the tier, and owes out $500 around the prison. That's equivalent to a year's pay on the other side of the wall. So Frankie is in imminent danger.

Frankie is in prison for the first time and is openly gay. So Frankie doesn't think anyone will beat the dog you-know-what out of him. He thinks this because he assumes the consequences and repercussions of fighting a gay man will be too embarrassing for the victor. People may misconstrue what they were fighting over, if you know what I mean.

Well, Frankie is dead wrong. This is not the streets. This is prison!

Blowing Smoke

So Frankie asked me if he could borrow $300 to pay off the gang who is going to do serious damage to him. Everyone knows I wear my heart on my sleeve, and that I'm a sucker for a sad story, but not this time. I have spotted Frankie over $200 since I've been here, and counted that for a loss. It always bewilders me how people can owe you and never intend to pay you back, and then ask to borrow again!

Now I can easily do much more harm to this desperate and impatient person, but I wasn't raised that way. I wish I could give every man in the prison a pack of cigarettes, and when they don't pay me back, they won't ask me again. Not Frankie. He's like a pussycat. You feed him once and he's coming back begging for life. So I made a pact with Holy Joe to take off my referee shirt and retire my whistle and stop trying to save people from their own poor choices. Frankie orders about $600 a month from canteen in nothing but cigarettes. No hygiene products, no food, no phone, just cigarettes. This is the bait he uses to lure in his blowfishes.

So Frankie must understand that the same thing that makes you laugh can also make you cry. So if I did see "Bubba" beating the brakes off Frankie last night, or if it was just a dream, I can only remember what my dad used to tell me, "A wise man sees only what he ought to see!" My advice to Frankie would be to stop blowing smoke and man up to your debt, because you know what they do with cigarette butts...step on them!

God's Giants

The apostle Paul said, "So I wouldn't get a big head, I was given the gift of handicap to keep me in constant touch with my limitations."

I started to think I had no weaknesses when I was a free man. I lost the very humility my parents instilled in me. Humility is not putting yourself down or denying your strengths. It's just being honest about your weaknesses and totally dependent on God. Notwithstanding my 6'10" frame, all of God's giants were weak people: Moses—his temper; Abraham—his fear; Peter—weak-willed; and David—murderer. Yet God transformed them into the humblest people on earth.

I must admit my weaknesses, be content with my weaknesses, glory in my weaknesses, and honestly share my weaknesses. Our weaknesses help encourage fellowship among believers. Christians, like snowflakes, are frail, but when they stick together they can stop traffic.

"And He said to me, 'My grace is sufficient for you, for My strength is made perfect in weakness.'" 2 Corinthians 12:9

Bad Bored

Dear Daddy,

It started last night with a miserable game of spades. I like to play cards because it's the only time that all the other inmates give me a break. The game is strictly for the purpose of camaraderie, but as of late, even that has been lost. So as soon as the card game was over, I went to retire for the evening. But first, I had to reassess my present situation. As far as my commitment to productivity goes, it is there. But my creativity is fading fast.

When I'm on the streets, I can see the fruits of my labor. If I build something, I can look at what I built. When I'm training for an upcoming basketball season, I can gauge my progress and improvement compared to other players and myself. But in prison, there is nothing to compare myself to. Even the black guys can't play dead in a cowboy movie.

I could say that I'm working on my patience, my relationship with God, or even staying away from partying. Not totally true, though. Not today anyway. My creativity doesn't have the passion I'm used to having in everything I do. When I'm feeling like myself, I'm living in Manhattan, taking on all comers. Today, I'm in a cabin sipping cabernet sauvignon, looking out on the lake thinking about how I will prepare the Porterhouse I just drove 20 miles into town to purchase. This decision takes no creativity, but it's not that easy.

My children love the city, and even though I shall soon be divorced, and have only weekend visitations, I would want to see them every day. It's simple. Either I buy a cabin close to NYC or just keep an apartment in NYC. Yesterday I had it all figured out. See, yesterday I was on fire with creativity. Today I'm dead wet with mundane.

I know myself way too well. I can program myself to be a robot for the rest of my prison bid. Pray, run, lift weights, sleep. That's how I created my skills for my profession. But my skills didn't make me a superstar. They just made me a very good basketball player. My passion was for creating my image—an outgoing person who never ran out of fuel with an imagination as strong as my shoulders.

I've never been in prison before. I've never been confined with 40 other men, everyday, 24/7. Doesn't matter who I try to surround myself with, unrealistic, dark, selfish people always invade. I can easily take the robotic way out, but my parents didn't raise me like that. Even if I tried to present myself that way, people wouldn't buy it.

I tried to pull away and become mechanical today, and people sensed that and I heard everyone's problems, and even worse, their uncreative solutions. There were women staffers yelling at me to smile and keep my head up, and new inmates on the tier pulling my personality like a chainsaw to get started.

I must realize that I am the most infamous prisoner in the history of the New Jersey Department of Corrections. Every prisoner in New Jersey knows my name.

Bad Bored

My parents taught me to learn everyone's name, also, and to treat them the way I would like to be treated. That's easy. I always greet everyone I come across and I know 80% of their names. But I'm bad bored. Meaning, this is getting old quick and I've only been here for 141 days—a little under five months. Karroway has been in prison for 25 years and he warned me this would happen. He added, "Even to someone with your charisma, Jay."

Just as I wrote that last sentence I found something (someone) to motivate me— Karroway. Another man just put a limitation on me. God put him in my life just to give me enough fuel to make it to tomorrow. Now that fuel will be burned up by 5:15 a.m., and I will find some more fuel named "Jesus" to keep me running on all cylinders until I get back to New York City to my passion, my family, and my creativity. So for now, I will burn out this fuel of self-doubt and negativity until my "Joy Juice" comes in the morning.

Love You, Big Daddy,
JW

P.S. Finish every day and be done with it. You have done what you could; some blunders and absurdities no doubt crept in; forget them as soon as you can. Tomorrow is a new day; you shall begin it serenely and with too high a spirit to be encumbered with your old nonsense.
~ Ralph Waldo Emerson

Tears of a Clown

I very rarely saw my Daddy actually pray, but when I did, he would look at me sort of embarrassed and shrug his shoulders and say, "Well, it don't hurt none!" That always made me laugh.

My mom, who is equally as funny, used stories to remind me of all the blessings I would miss out on if I didn't pray. Mommy used to tell me this story that always made me laugh:

> *Two men were in an airplane.*
> *Unfortunately, one man fell out.*
> *Fortunately, there was a haystack below him.*
> *Unfortunately, there was a pitchfork sticking*
> *up through it.*
> *Fortunately, he missed the pitchfork.*
> *Unfortunately, he also missed the haystack.*

My dad's mom, "Mama," always loved my smile, calling it "my most beautiful attire." Sitting here in my cell, I can almost hear her telling me to "Wear it, boy!" in her southern drawl. She always told me my smile could light up a room, and she even made me leave the room and re-enter if I ever came in a room without smiling. "Son, you make people feel good. So try it again, now. G'wan out the room and try that again with half a laugh on your pretty face, boy!"

"Okay, Mama, I will do that! I will leave the porch and run back in with the biggest grin on and laugh and yell at the top of my lungs, 'Mama! I *peeeeed* the *beeeeed*,' again!!"

My family always dealt with all of our tragedies by trying to find the good and the humor in situations. My parents lost three children very violently, but we prospered in our own way. I'm reading *David, A Man of Passion and Destiny* by Charles Swindoll and I find the humor in 1 Samuel 21:14-15.

Then Achish said to his servants, "Behold, you see the man (David) behaving as a madman. Why do you bring him to me? Do I lack madmen, that you have brought this one to act the madman in my presence? Shall this one come into my house?"

Basically, Achish screams, "I've got enough nuts in this court already! Don't bring me another one! Get rid of him!" David couldn't even find relief in his enemy's camp. Even the haters tossed him out!

David, like myself, had a position and he lost it. I had a wife and lost her. We both had and then lost a wise counselor—David lost Samuel and I lost my dad. David lost his friend Jonathan, I lost people who I thought were my friends. We both lost our self-respect.

They said David was walking around with spit hanging from his beard. I walked around with alcohol and sleeping pills hanging from my mouth. I remember going to accept my plea in front of the judge and hoping he would sentence me right there. I was in the "presence of my enemies" and he looked at this mess of a man and set me free for another 45 days. It's sad, but my family found the humor in it.

My family lives, loves, and laughs, although most of the time the laughing is at my expense. But as long as my parents are smiling, I will gladly bear the "Tears of a Clown."

Lie Down

"He maketh me to lie down in green pastures."
Psalm 23

Mr. Swindoll paraphrased the quote "A tree is best measured when it's down." Since I've been incarcerated, I now understand that more clearly. God sometimes uses solitude to train us. God taught David to learn all life's major lessons alone, sometimes as an outcast, before he could be trusted with responsibilities and rewards before the public. David remained responsible even when no one was looking. When you are herding sheep in the hot, cold, rainy weather and also have to fight off lions and bears with your bare hands, you become more diligent in all areas of your life.

I like to be busy and naturally resist being alone and quiet because I feel like I'm missing out or not accomplishing enough. But we all need time away from the crazy pace of daily life. Great poems are not written on crowded streets. The Psalmist said, "Be still and know that I am God." (Psalm 46:10).

I desire to be a man after God's own heart. When I do wrong, which is often, I want to admit it and repent immediately. Humility is a necessary ingredient to being a man after God's own heart. Even after Samuel anointed David with oil and made him king, David went back and tended his dad's sheep. I desire to be a man of integrity and know if I stay on the straight and narrow, while I'll forever be a work in progress, I can still aspire to be a man after God's own heart.

"He maketh me to lie down" which means sometimes God puts us on our backs to give us a chance to look up. Dr. Allen says, "Even the bed of an invalid may be a blessing in some ways if he takes advantage of it."

Both Sides

Chris, if you remember, is a white male who has "I Hate Niggers" and "White Power" stamped on his back. Well, since he's been on the unit we have spent some time together and come to find out, if he didn't have those tattoos I would never have perceived him as a racist. He's a funny man who had to step up to the plate to protect himself a couple of times and he did. But nothing to do with race. I truly think more times than not he wishes he had never defamed God's temple with his unanswered cries for love and attention.

He told me he hates his mom. I've heard a lot in prison but that's the scariest. Chris doesn't believe in God but I truly think he can be convinced. Chris thinks his race is just superior to others. Now, there are black inmates who think our race is superior. I don't *think*, I *know* that NO RACE is superior. *We can't judge a person by the color of their skin and not the content of their character*, says Martin Luther King.

Now, because all eyes are on me most of the time, I have been advised by some idiots that I should only talk to Chris when nobody is around. Almost like Nicodemus and Jesus. See, Nicodemus wanted to play both sides of the fence just in case Jesus was who He claimed to be. He wanted to have an in with Him, but if He wasn't, he didn't want to be seen in public with Him. Now, how can a high-ranking gang member and other fools ask me to watch who I hang out with? This African American gang leader has tortured my community tenfold what Chris will ever do.

See, I saw Chris in the hallway when I first arrived and he didn't return my good morning. So from that moment on I felt a certain way about him. Now after meeting him, I think he hates himself and is just immature. Okay, I keep stringing this out.

I worked in an office and Chris came in to get paroled and I interrupted the meeting to make the interviewer aware of the billboard of hate on his body. The person acknowledged that he was aware of it and told me Chris wouldn't get paroled because I should look at his files. I did go and illegally look at his "jacket" and he is a violent man. But it didn't say if he was violent against Jews, blacks, and gays, it just said "violent." Well, Chris was up for parole today and two members of the parole board postponed their meeting because one's African-American and the other's Jewish. I don't know if— well, I *do* know because I do carry a lot of influence, but the administration pretty much latched onto my misguided "I'm Superman and must save society from Chris" campaign. They told me, in so many words, that they were going to be as ignorant as Chris is, meaning jerk his parole around for one reason or another. I should have minded my own business. I'm as dumb as Chris. I judged someone I didn't even know. I haven't walked a mile in Chris' shoes.

I told Chris what I did because I spend a lot of time with him and I...well heck, I told him. Chris laughed as if to say, "I don't think it would have made a difference." Well, I'm just glad he's as ignorant as one of the tattoos on his body. Chris seems to be as good of a person as those I've let into my very small circle here in prison. But how would he act at his neighborhood bar if he were there with his friends and an African American walked in? Better yet, how would he treat my African American daughters? Man, these are questions that get my blood pressure up. Chris has spent 10 of his 28 years here on God's green earth in prison. Has he learned to get along with African Americans? Maybe I'm just mad at myself because I truly know I would've felt a certain way about him had our paths crossed prior to prison. But not anymore. Prison has taught me that I can't save the world and not to judge a book by its cover. I can go on and on about this but my hand hurts.

40 Men of Folly

The Prison Earlock

I sit "alone" in this prison of blocks and steel
with 40 men of folly at my side.
None I can trust, not even one
In None I care to confide.
They tell of high tales
Adventures never attended
Call the "bore" on their nonsense
Well now, look who's offended!
So I painfully listen
With the inevitable nod
Let's appear to mutually agree
All the time wondering
Why in God's good grace
this continually happens to me?
Just because my mind stalls
and may appear to be idle
My thoughts are still *mine,*
therefore, NOT yours to bridle!
My colleagues have become pitchmen
for their selfish ambitions!
So I grimace and nod
'til their next *Wow!* edition...
See, in prison it's nowhere to hide
with 40 men of folly at my side. ~JW

Crabs In A Basket

Good morning, Dad!

Everyone is a moon, and everyone has a dark side they never show anyone. In prison, your true colors will show. There are no sick days, no vacations, no "I'm running too late to come in today" excuses. Here you are with the same people 24 hours a day, seven days a week, 365 days a year.

Today Murdock is leaving on a self-requested transfer to another prison. His reason for leaving is because there is no central air-conditioning and the other inmates' smoking is jeopardizing his health. Well, that's what he wanted us to believe anyway.

Murdock is a funny guy, but a very dangerous man because he's an insecure person. Insecure people want you to feel the way they feel, which more often than not is miserable. I remember when you took my cousin and me crabbing one day in South Carolina to teach us this very lesson. I remember getting back to Grandma Elvira's house and watching you empty the day's fresh bushels into eight separate baskets on her porch. You instructed us to pay close attention to basket #3, which happened to be much more shallow than the rest. Every time a crab almost made it out of the basket and home free, another crab would reach up with its claws and pull the crab back down into the basket. It was like the crabs were saying, "Hey, dude! Get back here and suffer with all the rest of us!" You pointed out the fact that not all the crabs pulled that crab back down, just the envious ones.

Daddy, Murdock couldn't keep me down in his basket of misery because I've known what kind of a tattletale he is from the third day I arrived. The Bible says, *"As iron sharpens iron,"* so men sharpening men has been in full effect ever since then. I've known all along that he would tell the authorities any infraction I commit and I've used that for my benefit.

There are many times I'm miserable in here and I know some of the other prisoners hate me, but I must remember what President Nixon said, "Those who hate you don't win unless you hate them, and then destroy yourself."

So most of my time with Murdock was spent patronizing him from a distance. He would constantly put me on the phone with his mom. I only obliged because I understand how a mother can feel when her son is in prison. Now I'm patronizing myself. I'm just soft and can't say no to anyone, anyway. I would have spoken to a giraffe if Murdock had asked me to. Well, I'm working on saying no during my rehabilitation here in prison because for me to think is to say no.

Agatha Christie said it best, "If you love, you will suffer, and if you do not love, you do not know the meaning of a Christian life." So, Murdock just walked out of the gate of this prison for the last time. He will undoubtedly continue his ways, and also throw me into the fire in every conversation at his next destination. But I shall remain cool because Murdock left me his fan.

Ain't patronization great?
Miss you, Big Daddy,
Jay

P.S. Several years ago after a Bible study, Gayle King and I argued about whether it was "crabs in a basket" or "crabs in a barrel." I said "basket" because I've spent plenty of time crabbing in South Carolina and never once saw people hauling around giant barrels on their shoulders. The next time I saw Gayle she said she had someone look it up and turns out I was right. But so was she, according to the other inmates, who insist either one is correct. LOL

Your Own

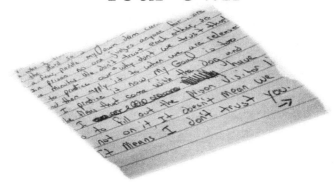

I might have done what they said I've done, but I don't have to be who they think I am. Trust me, I have done everything a man is supposed to do and not supposed to do. Sometimes good, sometimes not so good.

I remember finding a friend when I was 15 years old who wanted to be a basketball pro also. We would push each other toward this goal. His name was Brian. I totally trusted Brian because we had the same goals and he never leached off me. Even when it became evident that I was going to be a NBA star and he was respectfully going to get a real job in the business world, he never asked me for anything but friendship. I can look Brian in the face and say, "God bless the child who has his own."

I know people who went to school for half of their lives but have never accomplished half of the things they are jealous that I have accomplished, and will continue to accomplish. These people have told me that now that I'm in prison, I will fit right in. See, this is because they claim I like being the "Top of the Bottom." To this, I once again reiterate myself, *At least I'm at the*

Your Own

top of something!

Truly, there are not many goals that I've set for myself that I haven't accomplished. As a matter of fact, I mostly failed in things or with people that I didn't trust.

TRUST = LOVE to me. Some people might think I trusted you, but I never did. For the simple reason that I knew God didn't bless you to have "your own." So you needed "my own."

My mom is a given. She's my mother and I love her as much as my daddy, but my dad is the only person I truly trusted. My dad was my best friend. He would never hurt me. My dad always had his own and always gave me his own. See the difference? Daddy brought something to the party my whole life. Dad didn't just show up at the door, slip into the party, and think the party was for him.

My whole adult life I let lesser achieving self-centered people (for one reason or another) try to help me define who I am for their own benefit. I was a hostage of my own mistakes. Not no more! I'm in prison for a very long time and so be it. I live with 40 other so-called "bottom of the barrel" men in a space the size of an oversized living room.

See, for five months I've lived with the same people 24/7, everyday. Time will test these people. Nobody can "fake it till they make it" in these conditions for that long. The only person I've ever spent this much time with was my dad. On purpose! Because if I didn't trust you, I wouldn't be able to spend any consecutive amount of time with you. I would treat you like a prescription associate. I would take you in small dosages, a little at a time, only when necessary.

See, now I can't leave. I'm here with people I don't trust. I'm now very up front with those I trust. My daddy went to be with the Lord on November 10, 2009. Ever since then, I just do as he told me to do (regarding trust), "Like many, trust a few, paddle your own doggone canoe."

See, in prison, no one judges anyone for more than five minutes. We don't trust each other, so we get to practice our "why don't we trust that person?" and then apply it when we are released. Not me. I practice it now. My goal is to eliminate the fleas that come with the dog and start now. I have the say-so to fill out the prison visitor list. If you are not on it, it doesn't mean we dislike one another. It means I don't trust you.

I came into prison bewildered, confused, and unhealthy. I entered the stone walls and metal bars at 290 lbs. I'm now 240 lbs, content, controlled, and with better character. Am I still full of selfish ambitions? The same ambitions that paved the way right out of freedom? No, I'm just half full and when the tank hits empty, then— and *only then*— will Jesus release me from this time of clarity seeking.

I lost sight along the way to the NBA (natural born abilities) and while I was there I became insecure with my character and let slick-talking people I didn't trust into my circle. Shame on me. Shame, shame on me.

Hopefully I will stay until God gives them their own golden eggs or I will be released to tell them their goose is cooked.

See, I don't dislike all these people and the situations I put myself in, I can just do without them. God bless my new improved gift of discernment!

Come Back to Prison

Dear Daddy,

I read a book by Dr. Allen on the 23rd Psalm and instantly took to it. Psalm 23 talks about David, a shepherd just like us. But there are so many things that I never understood about sheep until I got to prison. Now there are no sheep here, but there are books, (LOL) one being the bestseller of all time.

You always taught me how things worked, but surprisingly, you never took the time to explain everything about sheep. That's because you knew I didn't really care about sheepherding. My passion was always basketball and you sternly explained (until I retired from the NBA), "You can play basketball after we tend to the chores." I never thought it was unusual to be feeding animals, building houses, or driving tractor-trailers in the morning, and then playing basketball in front of millions of people later that night.

Anyway, Daddy, Dr. Allen did a study on homeless children who didn't sleep well at night. He noticed they seemed restless and afraid. Finally, a psychologist hit on a solution. After the children were put to bed, they each received a slice of bread to hold. If they wanted more to eat, more was provided, but this particular slice was not to be eaten—it was just for them to hold. The slice of bread worked wonders and the children slept better because they went to sleep subconsciously knowing they would be fed the next day. That assurance that their needs would be provided for resulted in a calm, peaceful rest throughout the night.

Now back to farming. In the 23rd Psalm, David points out a similar connection in sheep. *The Lord is my Shepherd; I shall not want.* Instinctively, the sheep knows the shepherd has its grazing for the next day all figured out. So the sheep lies down in its fold with a piece of bread in its hand, so to speak.

Now here's something I have a hard time figuring out. Inmates who are released in July have told me they will be back in prison when winter approaches. You might be thinking what I thought, that these prisoners must have low self-esteem, with no acceptance, responsibility, or change in them; or that they just try to make the Bible fit their needs. But maybe the problem runs deeper. Paul says in Philippians, *My God shall supply all your needs,* and with that faith, we can work today without worrying about tomorrow. Now, I *know* God doesn't mean come back to prison when winter hits so you can be taken care of.

But if they don't come back, then who will I play basketball with? LOL.

Love you, Daddy!
Jayson

Sorrow

"He restores my soul."

Someone sent me a card and devotional about the 23rd Psalm. Inside the card were these words: Life ended for me somewhere during these years...through a slow process. I took years to stifle my faith; but now it is entirely gone...I am only a shell. Perhaps the shell... is gone!

During Bible study we studied how our mind is like the human body and it can be wounded. Sorrow is a wound. It's cuts deeply, but sorrow is a clean wound and will heal, unless something gets into the wound, such as bitterness, self-pity, or resentment.

Routine in prison is very important in keeping sane. I make sure I stick to my morning routine, which is 500 sit-ups and push-ups, stretching, and then prayer and Bible study. See, in prison, it is easy to become negative and hook up with the wrong crowd again. Misery loves company. So after the morning, when I arise to my routine, and start to feel the Holy Spirit, watch out world, here comes my commitment!

Some of my best games in the NBA were when I didn't think I even had the energy to play. Same goes for my walk with Jesus. Sometimes you have to put one foot in front of the other and do what you don't feel like doing. This might not sound totally Christian, but I often say to myself, *I already opened the Bible, I might as well make the best of it.*

I often tell my critics that I love peaks and valleys. Before prison I was more immature in my walk and I never prayed during the peaks. If I'm making every shot now, I continue to pray to make it last for as long as I can. When I go cold now, I am more confident in Jesus than I was when I couldn't miss.

I hope I'm finally moving from milk to meat with my walk with the Lord.

More Grace

Today a prisoner we shall call "Stinky" left. It brought me a sigh of relief when I heard he actually left the building.

Incarcerated for terroristic threats, Stinky was a Green Beret Marine who loved to lie about everything as much as he never wanted to take a shower. I could tell you all the lies this man told us, but my release date would be here before I ever finished writing. Stinky's ex-wife and three children were just killed in a car accident. At least that's what he told me and the other inmates when he wanted cigarettes. He brought out all the bells and whistles for that story and got three packs of smoke and tears that could water the grass in the Big Yard from me. Three days later we found out it was a lie and I forgave him, but the other inmates refused. Stinky was an indigent inmate who wasn't too proud to beg. After about the 40th pack of cigarettes (a new DOC record) I lent him, I asked him for a simple but necessary favor: type a letter for me. I patiently waited four days before asking him for the letter. Stinky replied, "I will get the mother f****** letter when I feel like giving you the mother f****** letter." Stinky just cursed out his only provider of food and cigarettes, not to mention the only bent ear for his never-ending lies.

So I reached my hand into his pocket and dragged him into the bathroom, his sneakers and the concrete were the only ones smoking now. Once in the privacy of the latrine he could better express his dislike for me, but before he could say, "Jay," something came over me and I grabbed him by the throat with one hand and lifted him nine feet in the air. My hand was there just to stop the air from entering his brain so I didn't have to hear another lie.

As Stinky was learning to float in midair, Holy Joe came running in and jumped up to grab my free arm, his 5'4 frame dangled above the ground like he was doing chin-ups. The preacher, who is supposed to be a man of God, started yelling at the top of his lungs, "Brother Jay you have too much to lose! Let the cracker down! He's a low-life redneck white bread trailer park trash, piece of s**t!" Wow, time to release Stinky and perform an exorcism on the preacher!

Stinky is proof that God still needs to work with my instantaneous reactions. But God showed more grace toward me by sending the only inmate who could stop me from not seeing my daughters for another five years. Thank you, Jesus. Again!

Oh yeah, turns out Stinky wasn't in here for terroristic threats; he was in here for sexually molesting his own children. So God showed him grace, also. Wow.

Back Pocket

It's been five months since I've had sneakers that fit my feet. My doctor and the prison doctor have approved the paperwork needed to attain proper footwear. This is not a luxury but a necessity. It's the law. My feet and now my pen both breathe revenge! Nice people aren't they? They richly deserve anything I can do to them. I tried not to make any noise about the situation, hoping compassion will show its head. Instead, the reality of walking around in pain for only God knows how long has showed its ugly head.

This man who just passed by my bunk doing his cell counting, he'll never listen to reason. His mind isn't constructed that way. While I reason with him in ideals and ideas, he isn't listening. He is thinking about which rule he'll quote to dismiss us. When he walks away you'll see the little codebook protruding from his back pocket. That's where he carries his mind, in his back pocket. When I attack the problem with intellectualism, I give away the advantage I have in my professional status. I'm going to have to kick him where he keeps his brain, in the region of his butt.

Power to the shoeless!!

Hirelings

For the month of July I have been taking a class on the Gospel of John. I'm both the professor and the student. I just read John 10:13: "The hireling flees because he is a hireling and does not care about the sheep."

The footnotes on this verse say, *The hireling is a hired shepherd, a mercenary, who tends the flock for his own interest. When a hired shepherd sees a wolf coming, he flees, not caring about the sheep.*

When my dad became an invalid and speechless for the last 742 days of his life, I went through an unbelievable amount of hirelings. I learned that these nurses were good for two weeks and then they no longer truly cared for my father. See verse 8: *"All who ever came before me are thieves and robbers, but the sheep did not hear him."*

Or even better, verse 5: *"Yet they will by no means follow a stranger, but will flee from him, for they do not know the voice of strangers."*

See for me, the "thief" (nurse) was the worst because this caregiver stole care from my daddy in secret. Then we had the just plain lazy nurse who was a robber. This nurse plundered openly with carelessness. The thief was the one who literally drove me to insomnia. I never knew if my daddy was being abused so I would never leave them alone.

My dad communicated with me through his eyes. So when a stranger (bad nurse, hireling) was among us, he wouldn't respond. Just like a sheep will not follow a stranger's voice, my daddy would do the same thing.

It took me until prison to forgive everyone who wanted to put Daddy in a nursing home with more hirelings. A good shepherd will lay down his own life for his own sheep. When my daddy died on November 10th, it was then and only then, that I knew it was time to come to prison and take care of my issues that lie before me. I had to get healthy. I was a hireling to the rest of the people I loved. Verse 16 implies that God has no favorites because He wishes that all be saved. I disagree with this. I think David was one of God's favorites. He was a good shepherd who tended to his sheep and would lay down his life for them, just like Christ laid down his life for me. God gave me a chance to voluntarily lay down my life for my daddy, but also to take up my life once again.

And given the opportunity, I would lay my life down for him again and again.

More Coffee?

*"Anyone Else Want Coffee With Their BULLS****?!"*

Insanity is often the logic of an accurate
mind over-tasked.
~Oliver Wendell Holmes,
The Autocrat of the Breakfast Table (1858)

I marvel at how much time an inmate has to better himself mentally, if he chooses to do so. Man's brain is, after all, the greatest natural resource. On the streets, others go to bed with their wives—we inmates, with our ideas. I have also discovered that all human evil comes from this: man's inability to sit still in a room. See, the state of an inmate is full of inconsistency, anxiety, and boredom. These three things in prison, mixed with selfishness and ego, is a recipe for destruction.

Here, within the confines of the Department of Corrections, something as minor as a pack of tuna and *I will pay you back when I feel like it* attitude can result in a tragedy like this true story:

The mess hall is where we inmates sit and eat while the corrections officers stay behind cages and bullet-

More Coffee?

proof glass so they can observe and watch us digest our food. One morning a fight broke out during breakfast. Nothing out of the ordinary in prison, but this fight, which was explained to me in graphic detail, was a gruesome reminder that you must be aware of your surroundings and potential dangers at all times.

A prisoner was hit in the back of the head and knocked to the floor by another inmate. As he lay there and the correction officers just watched, the aggressor began kicking and stomping on the man's face for five minutes straight. Then he straddled his back and jerked his torso up backward, breaking his spine.

As the man lay unconscious, he was dragged over to the coffee machine while no one interrupted this cowardly attack. Coffee, hot as fish grease, was released directly onto the face of the victim, until his face and neck melted completely off his body and the five-gallon container was as empty as his lungs.

Over 10 minutes after this murder, the guilty party calmly walked over to the bulletproof I'm-only-trained-to-observe glass, got down on his knees, folded his hands behind his head, and then screamed, "Anyone else want coffee with their bull****?" He then waited three more minutes before he was attended to. It was 10 more minutes before the victim received unnecessary medical treatment.

Stuff like this makes it impossible to reduce human society to one level. When you have inconsistency, boredom, and anxiety locked in a 6'x8' cell, you get insanity.

Chewed Out

"He leadeth me in the paths of righteousness for His name's sake."
Psalm 23

Today I read about how dumb sheep are. Most animals seem to have an inner compass that helps them find their way home no matter how lost they get. Not sheep. Sheep can't see 10 yards ahead of them and when given the opportunity, they will stray every time. Back in the days of David the Psalmist, the shepherds had a difficult job navigating the Palestinian fields when leading their sheep to pasture. They would guide the sheep along narrow and dangerous paths where one misstep could cause the simple-minded sheep to fall to their death.

Before I became too big for my britches, I used to make sure I hung out with guys about 20 years older than me. They were both my college coaches so I still bowed to their authority. Plus, they always wanted to go to dinner early and get home early. My coach Ron used to say, "The things I used to do all night, now take me all night to do!" So my elders, my shepherds, along with my Daddy, kept me on the right path of the straight and narrow.

The wheels started to come off my wagon when I let the hirelings tend to me. Remember, the hireling is someone who tends to the sheep for a day and doesn't have a relationship with them. So when I am released to freedom, I shall look up my old coach and beg him to help lead me in the paths of righteousness.

It's like that story about the cow that gets lost every Spring. How does this happen? "One tuft at a time." The cow starts nibbling on a tuft (patch) of green grass, and look up to find another, right next to a hole in the fence. Once finished, it looks up to see another tuft on the other side of the fence. The next thing you know, the cow has nibbled itself into being lost.

I do not deliberately set out to backslide, but if I do, please feel free to advise me as much as it takes, because no one is so empty as the man who has stopped walking with God and doesn't know it!

Comfort Zone Bullies

I can remember playing with players with the Nets that never really wanted to become a great team.

When you show people you have the ability to be great one game, they expect you to be as great every night. Two reasons why these selfish players didn't want to be great:

1. Pressure to perform every night.

2. Their comfort zone – see, they are used to blaming others and staying complacent.

It reminds me of what I learned today in Bible study about Moses. God presented Moses, who was now depressed about his next assignment, with his new territory. *Come and I will send you to Pharaoh that you may bring my people, the children of Israel, out of Egypt.*

Moses tried to avoid this mission. "Who am I that I should confront one of the world's most powerful men?" God had an answer for every one of Moses' excuses.

It has nothing to do with who you are, but who I am. I will be with you.

Comfort Zone Bullies

Once you break out of your comfort zone, it will get worse before you hit a utopia. Comfort zone bullies will attempt to push you back toward your comfort zone, trying to lead you back to so-called safety.

"You've never done that before," they cry.

"What about the money?"

"What will people say?"

"You're bound to fail."

"Just try crossing that line. You'll be sorry."

And like the author Mr. Wilkinson said, these will come from your family and friends.

Hit the Bricks

> "Bricks"
> The outside-
> the other side of the prison wall,
> can't wait to be on the bricks;
> Check it-30 days and I hit the bricks
> ~ Urban Dictionary; Prison Slang

In prison, somebody always reminds you of someone from back in your crew. If not, you try to convince yourself that they do, so you can rid yourself of the homesickness. Most of the time they have nothing in common but you lie to yourself to make it work so you can make "time." But when I do this and they are released from confinement, even though I'm happy for them, I still lose another pal from the old neighborhood. You know what? You start to feel like the guy in *The Green Mile*— or was it the mouse? Okay, that's sad, but when you start seeing guys hit freedom you know that your day is coming also. Better?

Out of the 900 inmates, here are just a few who have seen both sides of the gate during my incarceration.

Sydney Jones – He looked and sounded like my daddy and that was enough for me to wake up every morning at 5:15 am to share a cup of java with him.

Osman Turgay Yilmaz, "Oz" –– A man from Turkey whose broken English made him a shoo-in fit for the old prison movie Midnight Express. He punched me 15 times a day but made me laugh 16 times a day and I will take those numbers all day. Matt and I told him that we were gonna tie him up on his last night here. So "Oz" being a real life mercenary, outwitted two professional athletes by drugging us with Benadryl and tying us up. He gave Matt the world's biggest wedgie and short-sheeted his bunk as he slept. Since he liked me more, I just received another punch. But the funniest thing is we didn't know we were drugged until two hours after the FBI took him out of the prison. So once again, I exchanged one of his punches for the best "I gotcha suckers" laugh in prison history... well our prison history is only 5 ½ months... but still.

Lorenzo "Big Renz" Jackson – An inmate who loved to have intellectual debates, especially when he looked up the answers beforehand. Renz would just sit back and listen until somebody misquoted a fact, then he sounded a little like this: "What? What! What? Brotha' please! You don't even know what you talking 'bout Ninja! I'm telling you, Jack Johnson beat that honkey ass! It went 54 rounds! It was 1908 in Ireland! I'm telling you, I was there! Look Ninja, you got your hall pass? Then follow me. I got it in the book! The almanac – follow me Ninja!" Funny stuff. Renz always asked me to tell Matt stuff, but I think he actually meant it for me, not Matt. "Jay, go tell Matt he shouldn't play basketball with those gang members because they are jealous and will try to hurt him." Matt already experienced that, plus, I wouldn't let Matt see no harm. But since he claims he's been my #1 fan (long before I ever came to prison), I would oblige the old-timer and go play a non-contact sport. Renz left today after spending eight and a half years locked up and his mom thinks he still has two years remaining. I keep picturing his mom opening the door to her baby and then crying for joy. I replay that moment 100 times in my mind. That will keep me going for a while, because someday my mom will be opening that door with joy for me!

Gate: (1) Cell door. (PA) (2) Release, as in "30 days to the gate."

Gate Money: The small amount of money given a prisoner upon release.

Gate Time: When the doors to the cell are opened so that one can get in or out.

Gated Out: To be released from prison.

V.

Everybody thinks of changing humanity and nobody thinks of changing himself.
~ *Leo Tolstoy*

Ignorance Prevails
Two Wolves
Millstone
Happy Labor Day!
Mom, Look Who Came to Dinner!
Silly Questions
Attitude
Dump Trucks in Heaven
Stand Behind Me, Satan!
Black & White
Vanilla
Fan-Jacked
Window Gangsta
Dr. Gregory
Little White Lie

Ignorance Prevails

Where justice is denied, where poverty is enforced, where ignorance prevails, and where any one class is made to feel that society is an organized conspiracy to oppress, rob and degrade them, neither persons nor property will be safe.
~Fredrick Douglass

Dear Dad,

I've been called a racist before, along with everything else. The "everything else" doesn't bother me, but "racist" does because I have never looked at what part of society you come from or the color of your skin. Growing up in our biracial family gave me every reason to despise the racist mentality. Granddaddy lost his livelihood and almost lost you over the color of our skin and he never recovered. Your attempt to carve out redemption was burned to the ground by racists who wouldn't take no for an answer.

I've been called every name in the book by racists on both sides of our family, and by complete strangers, too. Since I was small, I've known that some white people will never accept me—but only tolerate me—because of my persona, charisma, and my lighter skin, which makes me look different from the "typical" black person. But most of all, they will not accept me because of my athletic abilities.

Black people are the folk who break my heart. They accuse me of being too friendly around whites. First of all, this plays on my intelligence, because I will never let anyone figure me out. To me, ignorance and boring behavior are signs of unintelligent or lazy people. I might be around whites so that I can keep the enemy closer. Never. White people will then figure me out. You used to say, "You should have education enough so that you won't have to look up to people, and then more education so that you will be wise enough not to look down on people." You raised me with those values, but I treat my friend as if he might become my enemy. For me to be prepared for war is one of the most effective means of preserving peace. Six months ago I wouldn't have even tried to preserve peace.

Inmates are a new one for me, Dad, but common sense and not being naive are not. Like you always said, prosperity makes friends, adversity tries them and it is a very hard undertaking to please everybody. Now, being sober 100% of the time, I shouldn't make that mistake again. There are no mistakes for me, just lessons.

Love you,
J

Two Wolves

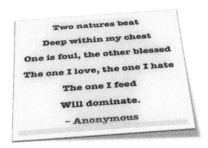

*Two natures beat
Deep within my chest
One is foul, the other blessed
The one I love, the one I hate
The one I feed
Will dominate.*

- Anonymous

Dear Daddy,

"Today is the 3rd of September, the day I always remember, the day that my daddy died." Those are the words to a song by the Temptations that was being poorly sung by another inmate a few minutes ago. I didn't stick to my routine this morning and am feeling a little out of sync and vulnerable. That song made me yearn for you, Daddy.

Dad, we always discussed wolves. These animals along with alligators fascinated us. Well, I have a confession to make. I have two wolves that live within me. Two hungry wolves, at that.

The first wolf is a pack wolf that goes out with a group of its peers— devouring, lusting, and manipulating its prey. It's quick to anger, aggressive, and a self-absorbed creature that is reckless for fun and adventure at any cost. This creature loves the wee hours of the morning because night vision is deceptive, allowing it to see and not be seen while running its demonic follies.

The other wolf is a lone wolf. It rarely hangs out with the pack. It's compassionate, loving, joyful, slow to anger— a wolf with integrity. This wolf doesn't like the dark because it has nothing to hide. This wolf has Christ-like characteristics.

But I have figured out my body will only allow one wolf to survive.

Which one will be victorious? The one I feed! Wow!

Love,

J

Millstone

In the little world in which children have their existence, whosoever brings them up, there is nothing so finely perceived and so finely felt, as injustice.
~Charles Dickens

Dear Big Daddy,

I have a picture of God's two greatest gifts above my bunk— Whizdom and Tryumph, my two angels, my daughters. Sometimes I wake up and feel some kind of way about not being able to protect them. Yesterday I became fearful and full of anxiety after we read Matthew 18:6 during our daily Bible Fellowship. "Whoever causes one of the little ones who believed in me to sin, it would be better for him to have a large millstone hung around his neck and to be drowned in the depths of the sea."

Hearing that verse set me off and immediately after our study, I expressed my objection about a person Matt jails with, saying something like, "This guy is bad people." Basically, I think Matt's friend is a child molester—just a gut feeling—and I questioned why he wasn't trying to correct this man or make him confess his sins to us and try to improve.

There are several underlying factors that have more to do with me and my selfish ambitions than they have to do with Matt and his friend.

First, I'm selfishly incarcerated and am not able to protect my daughters. Second, why does he need to confess to us? Who are we? He first needs to confess to God. I was wrong to blame Matt for his friend's possible indiscretions, but when I read that passage I thought the timing was great, if nothing else.

See, I'm scared that I'm not ready to come out of the oven yet (be released from prison). If this man was to take the innocence of my daughters then I would make sure that Matthew 18:6 was not just hypothetical. Understandably, if I were to react in such a selfish manner, I would be returned to prison and my angels would have no one to counsel or protect them for life!

God, I'm serious. Please give me the strength and ability to forgive ALL who do evil to my family.

Daddy, I cry when I write this because I need a miracle for me not to do harm to the perpetrator in these kinds of situations. Please send help quickly, Dad!

I have since apologized to Matt, who totally understands because he has someone in his life about the same age that he left unprotected in our eyes. But in God's eyes, we don't give Him due credit for being our One and Only Protector.

Love You, Pop,
Jayson

Happy Labor Day!

Everybody ought to do at least two things each day that he hates to do, just for practice.
~William James

Dear Dad,

Today is Labor Day and you wouldn't believe it. Dad, it sounds like the Fourth of July mixed in with New Year's Eve. To be honest, half of these prisoners don't know it's Labor Day and the other half don't know what Labor Day is.

Dad, the other half (yes, another half! LOL) never had a real job. Labor disgraces no man; unfortunately, you occasionally find that men disgrace labor.

The prison is slow today because the administrators are off. But the inhabitants are not slow to anger. Karroway, who has spent 30 of his 52 years in prison, is usually the person who makes sure our tier is clean and in order. Karroway had to attend court this week so chaos has ensued. We are not building rockets, we're cleaning toilets. But it's not about tier sanitation and

Clorox, it's about power. And the lust for power is the strongest of all passions.

See, in prison, being in charge of something gives you authority. And if you wish to know who a man really is, place him in authority. With an ignorant person now in charge, here comes the yelling and shouting. That's when these guys sound like a bunch of drunken sailors trying to kill one another. I want to see them fight the way they shout. All shout, no action.

So instead of doing physical harm to these gang-bangers, I will remember what you taught me about action—*The shortest answer is doing.* So I picked up the sponge and the Clorox and looked over at Matt for some assistance, knowing he should be proud of the way I diffused the situation.

"Matt, let's knock out this bathroom sanitation real quick."

Matt took the covers off his face just long enough to give me man's greatest laborsaving device: "I have a backache."

Well, Dad, Happy Labor Day and yeah, before I forget, today makes 240 days or eight months of being sober. I know you knew I could do both—not kick their butts over the bathroom and stay sober.

Dad, just think for a second. Imagine if I was drinking and these guys would have been yelling about the bathroom like this! Now I *know* Jesus knows what He's doing.

Love you, Dad.
JW

Mom, Look Who Came to Dinner!

Dear Mom,

I'm writing you this letter because you worry so much about me while I'm in prison. You can't see how well I'm getting along. If I tried to explain every aspect of prison life you would become overly concerned and worry yourself sick, and I need you here in the flesh with me, Mommy. I love you, Mommy! So much love for you, Mom.

Okay, Mom, remember when someone stole my custom-made Go Cart and the signs off the gates of our New Jersey home? Remember we didn't prosecute because we didn't need any more media coverage? Well, "K" is here. On my tier. Just a few feet away as I write this letter to you, Mom. Now, I'm not going to make this melodramatic and you don't have to preach to me. You never did. Your actions spoke for themselves. You always set an awesome example. No harm will come to this thief from me—not just because I love you and my children and want to get home to you all, but because I no longer have anything to prove to anyone—including myself. Yes, Mother, finally.

I'm surrounded by some of the largest, strongest, most medieval, and Satanic cowards in prison society. Not all (Mom, calm down!), but *most*. And because I ate all my cereal, and the vegetables you cooked for me every day, I can easily crush them silly. That's the sweetest way I can put it, Mom. Remember, I'm still in here, and "slang" is half the battle with some of these fools.

Mom, K laughingly told me how funny he thinks it is—him stealing and selling our stuff on eBay. Yes, Mom, and he's also a racist so I'm pretty sure he doesn't approve of your interracial marriage with Dad. I'm not trying to rally the troops to get your permission to "deal" with him. Although, if you do write me back, send me that wooden spoon you broke over my head every week and I will gladly share that love with K the Thief!

Okay Mom, as he told me that story about eBay, I gave him the same look you gave me when I was an altar boy and you caught me sleeping during the third service. Then I became practical and took a vigorous five-mile walk around the yard. It did more good for an unhappy, but otherwise healthy basketball player than all the medicine and psychology in the world. You were right, Mommy Dearest! Proverbs 22:6 says, *"Train up a child in the way he should go, and when he is old he will not turn from it."*

Talk to you tonight. The thief also has a mom and he shall return to her unharmed. I promise!

Love You,

J

Silly Questions

Dear Jesus,

Before my trial and tribulations, I would think of the Bible often, but mostly with silly questions. Being a Catholic meant routine to me, not commitment. You can be less than a Christian all week long and then go to confession and receive a clean slate from a mere man. Wow.

Well, not anymore. The days of a quick fix and, *Where in the Bible did they talk about dinosaurs?* are gone. I don't need a man to mediate between God and me. In basketball, we call that an agent. If I have a question, I won't ask the invention itself (the device)—I will ask the person who invented it.

I remember going to so-called prophets or fortune-tellers during my trial. Lord, forgive me for this desperate act! When I'm standing in line at the summer's blockbuster movie, do I ask the person coming out the theatre what happened at the end? No! Because then it truly wouldn't be worth seeing, or better yet, in my mind I would constantly be trying to modify the ending for my benefit.

It's simple. My movie (life) can end exactly the way I want it to by just believing in You and obeying You, Jesus. But most of all, by entrusting my future to You, rather than asking someone else how it's gonna play out.

Just *Be still and know that He is God*. Yes, *God*—as in, the guy who invented Steven Spielberg.

Love,
Jayson

Attitude

Of all delusions perhaps none is so great as the
thought that our past has ruined our present, that the
evils we have done, the mistakes we have committed,
have made all further Hope impossible.
~ Archbishop Goodie

Dear Dad,

I've been in prison for 242 days now and let me tell you something I've observed. There is little difference in people—the little difference is attitude. Is the glass half full or half empty?

The most important decision I can make every day is my attitude. It is more important than my past, my pain, my reputation, my finances, and any situation I find myself in. Attitude can single-handedly block my road to joy and fill me with anxiety and insecurity. It alone fuels my fire or destroys my faith. When my attitude is firing on all cylinders, and with God's blessings,

I can change the world.

Some "evangelist" might say I was unfortunate enough to watch you gamble at cards, but even when you lost, you taught me to imitate you as if you had won. You knew when to walk away and you had a positive attitude at all times.

You taught all of your boys how to build our own homes. When I was 15 years old I promised you I could build one without your assistance, and then I went out and got real busy finding out how to do it. The only way I wouldn't have been able to build that house is if I told myself that I couldn't.

I remember you telling me about a guy you worked with who had a "glass half empty" attitude. He was lazy, insecure, and had an excuse for anything and everything concerning hard work. You once told me if you took a quarter from your pocket and threw it off the Empire State Building and it hit him on the head, it would seriously injure him. Talk about getting your money's worth. We both laughed and I totally understood the point you were making about attitude. We become what we think about all the time.

I probably will write about attitude every so often to remind myself about having a positive attitude if I'm going to make it in prison. I will not lie. It really *has* felt like 242 days incarcerated, but it could have also felt like 1242 days.

So tighten up, Big Fella!

We have a world to conquer in *His* name.

Love,
Your favorite criminal
Inmate #780161B/652698

Dump Trucks In Heaven

My mommy used to use three things to get me to obey her. One, the wooden spoon, or should I say spoons, because they didn't last but one good lick. The second was, "You wait until your father gets home!" And the third was a parable from the Bible with a twist of Mommy love.

A lil' boy who wouldn't say his prayers when his mommy asked him to was called to Heaven to drive dump trucks for Jesus. (My mom knew I loved Tonka toy dump trucks, but that I loved being with my mom and dad more.)

So the lil' boy who wouldn't say his prayers was called up to Heaven. St. Peter said, 'Jayson, we only have one rule up here and that is that you never go into that warehouse over there.'

'Okay,' Jayson answered. 'But when do I get to see my parents?'

'Not for a long time, Lad,' St. Peter answered firmly. 'Now go off and help Jesus make the road of the straight and narrow.'

Jayson loved driving trucks for Jesus, but missed his parents dearly. One day, Jayson stopped the dump truck right in front of the warehouse he was forbidden to enter and you know what Jayson did, don't you, Jayson?

"Yes, Mommy. I didn't follow instructions," I would answer in a *I know... I know...*tone.

Mommy nods her head in agreement and continues.

Well, Jayson saw tons of huge Christmas boxes with bows, and wrappings, and each one was marked with someone's name. Jayson ran around the warehouse for days until he finally found a box that read, 'Jayson Scott Williams.' Right before Jayson went to open it, a stern voice echoed from right behind him. 'I wouldn't open that if I were you,' St. Peter said.

Again, Jayson not following the rules, jumped up there and opened the box, only to find hundreds more boxes inside. He grabbed the biggest one he could find and opened it to find an envelope inside. Jayson opened the envelope like the Jayson of old—just shook the card to see if any money would fall out, not even bothering to fake like he was reading the card—and sure enough, no money came out. So Jayson looked at St. Peter with a look of disappointment. 'What are all these envelopes? Hundreds of them?'

St. Peter said, 'Read the card that's in your hand.'

'Okay,' Jayson said, obediently. Then he read the card aloud. 'Three brand new dump trucks on earth: one for Jayson, one for Mommy, and one for Daddy.'

Jayson became all excited, but confused. As Jayson stood there, scratching his head, St. Peter took the card and threw it back in the box and put it back on the shelf. St. Peter looked at Jayson and said, 'See JW? All those hundreds and hundreds of what you thought were presents were blessings. But since you didn't say your prayers every night and ask for them, we just stored them up here.'

I would look at my mom and then jump out of her

arms and down onto my knees and ask God for all the blessings I could, one being, "Can I please stay with Mommy and Daddy forever?"

Mom didn't need a spoon or idle threats about Daddy to get me to pray anymore, just that beautiful parable.

Stand Behind Me, Satan!

Beware of people who are close to you. I remember my pastor telling me that seven years ago when I started seminary. He warned me that even those who encouraged me to pursue a closer relationship with God could become envious of my newfound knowledge of the Bible.

Wow, why? I thought to myself. Then I dismissed it. But as soon as I tried to discuss the Word with my loved ones, they became defensive and short with me. See, I didn't have to listen to *their* version of the Bible anymore, their opinions and interpretations, because I was now going straight to God's Word for my information. When I see how something works (like the Bible), I like to learn it and work it. Once you go to the source, the Bible, you can no longer be manipulated by ideas, opinions, and philosophies. I became more on fire for Jesus than my loved ones. Well, at least I spent more time wanting to know more about Him. I can't say how on fire for Jesus my loved ones were.

The same thing happens in prison. As soon as you get here, the staff (mostly corrections officers) tries to

Stand Behind Me, Satan!

teach you how to do jail. This one CO in particular had nothing but manipulative evil in her heart. Well, that's the way it seemed to me, anyway. She would try to show you the ropes, not to help you survive, but to help you become dependent—on her. Her intentions were spurious at best. Once she figured out that I wasn't going to have a problem and that I had a good heart, she gradually became angry. I didn't "need" her and I think she likes to be "needed" in order to feel significant.

She tries to make jail tough for you any evil way she can, from telling you how much trouble she saves you from to trying to start chaos and strife between your fellow inmates. Once you shout, *Stand behind me, Satan!* (in your head) every time you come in contact with this wretch, and then ignore her, *Uh Oh!* Here comes more trouble!

I've only been upset in prison a few times, but this one angered me a lot, mostly because I'm always nice to this malcontent of a person, like I am with everyone else. Nice to the point where other inmates ask me why. I'm always making excuses for her actions and she doesn't even know it. Corrections officers go home, prisoners don't. Get my drift? It can be very dangerous standing up for the staff.

I tell you the truth, I went to my bunk and asked Jesus to first make it "no," not "slow" to anger. Then I asked my Lord to forgive this empty soul of a staff member. One hour later, I forgot about her transgressions and went to church. I studied my Bible, and it moved me from milk to meat. Thank you, God, that I'm learning more about the Bible, which therefore teaches me how to deal with envious lost souls.

Keep me from evil and even though I feel deep sympathy for this hollow shell of a person, I'd rather just pray for her and keep her afar.

Black & White

My mother said I must always be intolerant of ignorance but understanding of illiteracy. That some people, unable to go to school, were more educated and more intelligent than college professors.
~ Maya Angelou

Dear Daddy,

Inmates are like the moon and have a dark side that they never show to anybody. But prison shows that side. Locked up 24/7, 365 days a year—no lie can last that long. In this prison, Mid-State Correctional Facility, blacks don't bother whites, but I've been made aware that if I was at an all-white prison, even the whites who surround me now would try to harm me.

Our tier here is semi-segregated because of the actions of just a few. The back of the tier where I sleep is black, the front is white. I've been using the front because Matt and I work up there because it's quieter, no card playing, TV, or smoking. In the last month, there have been some bed changes, bringing in a few who have tried to move me and my writing to the back. So, unlike me, I move to the back. Not because I'm scared or tired of fighting or faking it, but because I don't own the front and those involved will not listen to reason—"reason" (in here) always means what someone else has to say. I didn't want to write anything about racism in my letters, but I always want to remember these specific events and dates.

I have two African American daughters. Now you can understand why I feel a certain way about racism. As I just wrote that last sentence, two pro-black inmates said something to the effect of, "I told you! Now you are learning about white people. You have moved to the back of the bus (tier) again." I quickly laughed at that nonsense for fear of having to cry with anger. It's just this simple: "I do not think much of a man who is not wiser today than he was yesterday." I will continue to be a good-hearted person because I have come to wisdom through failures. I will keep my mind on the big prize and that's how I am. I have to get mentally healthy so I can help others. But I lay it down as fact that if all men knew what others said of them, there would not be four friends in the world.

    Miss you, Daddy,
    Jayson

Vanilla

> Great tranquility of heart is his who cares
> for neither praise nor blame.
> ~Thomas à Kempis

Dad,

I'm concerned with how at peace and in stride I am taking everything. I read L.B. Cowman's daily devotional, and it was exactly what I wanted to discuss with you. First, the journal said, "God does not want us to be like greenhouse plants which are sheltered from rough weather, but like storm-beaten oaks which have weathered the storm."

Dad, you know since I was 14 years old I've always taken on the emotional stress of the family. Well, for 25 years, I have not felt more at peace than I do now. Not only at peace, but prepared. Prepared for the next storm. I feel so prepared Dad that I have become almost robotic. Nothing seems to agitate me or even better (or worse?), I'm not uneasy with any situation my foes might try to put me in. This— as your son and a professional athlete— should be what I want, and it is. What I'm attempting to say is that I have learned that people who loved me— or I should say the people who *depended on* me— are doing it by themselves without me.

So for me to have thought for even a minute that they would self-destruct without me shows how overrated I am in my own mind. I thought that if people depended on me more they would also love me more. That has ceased. This is where the robotic Jayson has arrived. I'm no longer concerned or worried about their follies and tribulations, or mine either.

Dad, I'm not angry or envious that people are doing well without me. I only care to be loved by Mom and by my daughters, Tryumph and Whizdom, but no one else. I'm actually enjoying being robotic, for lack of a better word. Life is "vanilla"—except for the very few attributes of funny that I will let just acquaintances now enjoy.

Dad, I love the joy and peace God is giving me, but it's almost like the ceiling of complacency. I like this address and I will trust in God that it's just another step forward toward weathering future storms. But today, Dad, I feel I'm becoming more like the mighty oak that is planted by the river and cannot be moved.

Love you,
Jayson

Fan - Jacked!

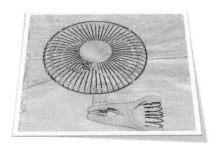

I'll give you some symptoms of a sign that your faith is deteriorating. Whenever you face all of your problems and you trust only your plans to get you out, it is a sign that your faith is deteriorating.
~ T.D. Jakes

Dear Dad,

Do you remember Johnny Johnson, the heavyweight champion in prison with me? He beat up a gang member who tried to bully him. Well, at 52 years of age, he still requires regular catnaps several times a day. So yesterday, while the champ was resting, I saw him reach up to turn on his personal fan. (The thing is a six-inch Mercedes in the prison economy.) When it didn't respond, he flipped the power switch a second time. Still nothing. So he got off his bunk to look for another outlet and when that didn't work, he shook the fan violently while cursing it out. Finally, using our version of the Swiss Army Knife (toenail clippers,) he pried the fan open to discover that it won't be working again anytime soon. The motor was stolen.

Dad, it was so funny to see the expression on his face. It was the same one you had when they stole the motor our of your '73 Thunderbird. Hysterical.

Well, needless to say, the champ didn't find the humor in being fan-jacked. But instead of beating the brakes off of half the prison, he went straight to the notes I write him every morning from the Gospel of John. After a minute or so, he stood up and cleared his throat to address all of the prisoners on our tier: "He who steals a fan motor will also steal an ox." And then he sat back down and opened his Bible to the Book of John.

I think I just watched a parable unfold. Johnny treated the fan like I treated God, only interested in our relationship when something goes wrong. I'm like a fair-weather friend. And I still get impatient when I don't think He hears me or when He doesn't do what I think He should do. I try all my own ways to get what I'm after, but even after all the shaking, yelling, hitting—I'm still hot, and my fan is still broken. I have to keep reminding myself that the fan will never work without the motor. Jesus is my motor and if I don't have Him, you can plug me in anywhere and I will never work for His purpose.

Love and miss you,
Jayson

Window Gangsta

Often, when I am running in the yard I will hear someone calling my name from the prison windows. It will most likely be a dumb question that they know the answer to or that has no value whatsoever. They do this so they can say they've met me and have a relationship with me.

Yesterday, one of the "window gangsta" (as I not so pleasantly call them) shouted, "Yo, Jay Dub, do you know Michael Jackson?" I stopped my stride and went over to explain that, "No, I don't know the King of Pop, but I do know the King of the World, Jesus." Yes, I have met Michael Jackson several times but I do not know him. I have never had a meaningful conversation with him. Mr. Jackson probably doesn't want to know me. Now that *God* character, *He* wants me for a close friend.

The Bible says that He is a God who is passionate about his relationship with you. Knowing and loving God is our greatest privilege and being known and loved is God's greatest pleasure.

So please don't boast about knowing an athlete when the Bible says, "He made the entire human race and made the earth hospitable, with plenty of time and space for living so we could seek after God, and not just grope around in the dark but actually find Him." (Acts 17:26-27 MSG)

And you know I can't end this journal without a little story.

I remember speaking to the great sports star Mickey Mantle. He told me about a recurring nightmare. "Sorry Mickey," the Lord said, "but I wanted to give you the word personally. You can't go to Heaven because of the way you acted down on earth, but would you mind signing a dozen baseballs?"

Dr. Gregory

It is easy to be pleasant
when life flows by like a song,
but the man worthwhile
is the one who will smile
when everything goes dead wrong.
For the test of the heart is trouble,
and it always comes with years,
and the smile that is worth
the praises of earth,
is the smile that shines
through the tears.
~ Irish Saying

Dear Dad,

I'm sorry for focusing so much on me in the letters and not my siblings, even though I'm your favorite. Just kidding. Not really. Do you remember when Gregory Williams, your second child, who was about to become a doctor, was telling this joke? LOL. Wow.

Jayson once asked God how long a million years was to Him. God replied, "A million years to me is just like a minute in your time."

Then Jayson asked God what a million dollars was to Him. God replied, "A million dollars to me is just like a single penny to you."

So Jayson got his courage up and asked, "God, could

Dr. Gregory

I have one of your pennies?"

God smiled and replied, "Certainly, just a minute."

Daddy, I told my brother that story 20 times and he messed it up every time, except the night of his graduation. He became a doctor with his Ph.D. that night and a great joke teller at the same time, for that night anyway. I was so nervous when he started that joke and so were you. I guess they are right, Dad, success is 99% failure. Dr. Reverend Gregory Williams got the 1% that night. It doesn't matter how much pain the Williams family has been through, we always find time to live, laugh, and love.

I've been in prison for almost 300 days now and if you were with me, Dad, we would be laughing and loving. Now I know you are here with me spiritually and we do laugh, but I have to be more guarded with my laugh these days. If the warden sees me walking around laughing, and only I can see you, I'll be sent to lock-up. LOL.

Daddy, those who can't laugh at themselves leave the job to others.

Okay, enough about me, the dark sheep of the family. Let's talk about Dr. Gregory Williams some more. Somebody should have told him that the story you told about Great Granddaddy was a folk story. If they had Google 20 years ago, you and I would have run straight out of Bethune Cookman College when Dr. Gregory told the following lie (unknowingly) that had the audience in tears, and us nervously biting a hole in our lips, holding back belly laughter.

"My Great Granddaddy had devoted his life to helping other blacks and whites who were underprivileged. He was also a doctor." Dad, do you remember the looks on our faces when we realized Dr. Gregory believed that story you told him about Great Granddad? LOL. Okay, back to Dr. Gregory's speech.

"Great Granddad, who was also called Dr. Williams,

lived over a liquor store in the poorest section of South Carolina. In front of the liquor store was a sign that read, Dr. Williams is upstairs. When he died, he had no money and neither did our family. He had never asked for payment from anyone he ever treated. So family and friends scraped enough money to bury the good doctor, but they had no money for Granddaddy's tombstone. Someone came up with the idea to take the sign from in front of the liquor store and nail it to a post over his grave. It made a lovely epitaph: Dr. Williams is upstairs.

LOL. Dad, since I'm coming clean to you in our letters, can I please tell my brother you made that parable up?

Love you, Daddy,
Jayson

Little White Lie

In speaking the words, you release the shame. ~ Oprah

Good Morning, Dad,

Do you remember when you and Mom were first courting each other? Mom told me that you didn't pick her up one night and you blamed it on your "birthday hangover." Dad, you said that your birthday was on August 26th. We believed you. I believed you.

Dad, I'm managing my tone to you as I write this letter, because if I don't, it will come to an abrupt end. By now Dad, you know I would never talk to you as if I were the parent, but I believe as our friendship and love for one another continues to grow, I can sometimes talk to you like this. So with all due respect, and if this is okay, I will continue.

On August 26, 1978, Uncle Vince was showing my cousin and me his gold bracelet, which had as many gadgets on it as a pocket Swiss Army knife. We were in awe. Uncle Vince then showed us a fifth of scotch and a glass to put it in. Then my very own uncle, your brother, showed us a couple of things 10-year-old boys should never know.

Dad, I can't remember. I've tried but I can't remember exactly what perverted acts went on, but these are some things I do remember.

I remember you weren't in South Carolina when this happened. You were in New York City celebrating your other brother's birthday on August 26th. That's whose birthday it really was. You guys weren't twins. But see where I'm going with this little white lie, Dad?

I remember Mom was in New York City, too. I was staying with Grandma Elvira in South Carolina.

I remember Uncle Vince gave me $5 to drink a whole glass of scotch straight down.

I remember that once my cousin and I returned home from Uncle Vince's hotel room, I was placed in Grandma's living room for two days while I recovered from the "overdose." Nobody was ever allowed to sit—let alone lay—in that room.

I remember family members manipulating me into believing that I was a bad child for drinking alcohol. And when we called you that day on the phone, that's all we would focus on. Alcohol, not molestation!

I remember telling you I drank alcohol and expecting the scolding that was going to come from it. But for some reason, you weren't focused on me anymore. I thought you were so ashamed of me and that's why you never talked to me about it. Or that's why you and I never talked about sex period—hoping to never accidentally brush against that scab that would ooze out acts of a sick man and two innocent children. Your own brother, Dad! Geez!

I remember overhearing conversations, only bits and pieces. Grandma telling Uncle Vince once that he should "go from here." And something about Granddaddy tying him to a tree when he was 12, saying he was going to kill him when he returned from logging that day.

I remember that this was the first time Uncle Vince had returned home in 40 years. And he went and did the unthinkable. Revenge against you and his sister? I don't know, Dad. But even then, I didn't want to get you upset or get Uncle Vince in trouble. I just wanted everybody to be a normal family.

I remember you rushed right to South Carolina, immediately after hearing the news. Meanwhile, Uncle Vince rushed right back to New York City.

I remember seeing how scared you looked for me, but I also saw red in your eyes.

I remember my cousin's mom grabbing her pistol and driving to New York City like it was an ordinary trip to the neighborhood nightspot.

I remember secret family meetings and you being ever so cautious of me not hearing them.

I remember not being able to tell Mom because maybe you two would get divorced.

I remember hearing Grandma screaming on the phone because Auntie went and shot up Uncle Vince's vacant apartment.

I remember Uncle Vince returning to South Carolina again 20 years later and resuming his acts. This time he received eight years in prison.

And finally, *June 15th*.

That's your real birthday, Dad. *June 15th*, not August 26th. That little white lie brought tremendous pain to everyone, man. I know you would have been with us on August 26th if you weren't pretending it was your birthday.

Well, it took 32 years to have this conversation. Dad, please respect my tone of voice on this one. But that was your fault. Not mine! Yours!

I'm glad we had this conversation, Dad. I forgive you and Uncle Vince. My cousin and I always talked about forgiving him and we have. Only a demon would hurt a child, and it would take a couple of saints to forgive, and hopefully now forget.

    Talk to you after breakfast, Dad.
Tone back to normal.
No more little white lies.

Love,
J

    P.S. I found out when your real birthday was when I was in my thirties and we were at the DMV together getting your license renewed. I looked over your shoulder and saw the date on your paperwork. Mom found out years later (not by me) but you went to your grave believing you had fooled us all.

VI.

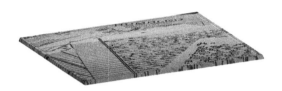

Adversity has ever been considered as the state in which a man most easily becomes acquainted with himself, being free from flatterers.
~ *Samuel Johnson*

Heroes & Villains
This is My Season
Oxymoron
Tantrums
No Explanations!
Like a Child
New Jail Smell
Let it Rain!
Help Wanted
Cobwebs & Cables
Can't Be Ruined
Lessons at Eight
In a Puddle
Just Do Me
Self
Down the Ladder
Egotistical, But True!
Courage

Heroes & Villains

Since wars begin in the minds of men,
it is in the minds of men that the defenses
of peace must be constructed.
~ UNESCO Constitution

Dear Dad,

Another thing we always had in common was our leadership. Even in prison, I am a leader because of my accomplishments on the other side of the barbed wire. And I've heard just about every insult that goes along with the job. But I keep in mind what you taught me about being kicked in the rear—it probably means you're out in front.

Some inmates are intimidated by my size, period. Now you mix that in with, *Maybe when he gets mad he's a killer...* most will error on the side of caution. See, in the real world, one murder makes you a villain and millions, a hero. Well, in here, being a killer somehow makes you a leader. What I tell these misinformed inmates is that you cannot put the same shoe on every foot. I had an accident plain and simple. But worse than that, I tried to cover it up like a coward.

See Dad, since "everyone's innocent" in here, I have learned that not every question deserves an answer. I'm a leader simply because I'm capable of touching their hearts. I also know where I want to go, then I get up, and I go. But in prison, everyone wants to let you know that they, too, could be a leader but they don't want the BS that goes with it. *Right!* Now that's BS!

Lao Tzu said, "A leader is best when people barely know he exists, when his work is done, his aim fulfilled, they will say: we did it ourselves." If this gang member who doesn't want the BS had said it like that, he would have been correct. And since we're on the topic of gangs and leaders, they can't get it right in prison either. You hear of stabbings and beatings all the time from the #2 leader because he wants to be #1, also. They must realize that when two men are on a horse, one must ride behind. You used to tell me that most wealthy people wouldn't want to be president because they that govern the most make the least noise. The wealthy can make all the laws from the comfort of anonymity. No jail, no negative feedback.

Dad, without boasting, I know that I can beat the brakes off of any of my peers. But in prison and with my stature, it's not about muscle. It's about getting along with people. Now, my peer Matthew can also take care of himself, not to my capacity, but he doesn't care at times. He will take on all comers. The problem is, in here they don't come one at a time because they are cowards. They come ten deep with shanks. Matt is a leader, but I have more experience in life and can recognize a situation before it becomes an emergency. Even so, I try to keep my fears to myself and share my smart courage with him. In the military, they require all leaders to be pompous. In prison, it will get you killed.

Dad, you always reminded me that experience is a good, but very expensive teacher. So with Matthew, we try to learn with caution, because we will never forget these lessons. Our lives depend on it.

Till tomorrow Dad, love you.
Jayson

This Is My Season

It's very simple. There's only one requirement
of any of us, and that is to be courageous. Because
courage, as you might know, defines all other human
behavior. And, I believe - because I've done a little of
this myself - pretending to be courageous is just as
good as the real thing.
~ David Letterman

Dear Daddy,

It's September 14th and I remember this type of weather. It was never appealing to me. I think you enjoyed it more because you knew it was time for me to go back to school and get out of your hair for the next nine months.

I never really could understand it, but it could be 85 degrees around Labor Day and I could always detect the cold front. It reminded me of fool's gold. I always became anxious because I knew I wouldn't be with you and that I had to go back to school. School wasn't all that necessary for me, in my way of thinking. Then again, I almost just misspelled "necessary" so maybe I did need more schooling. But I remember looking at all the other children as unbalanced. Maybe their dads made them all sit around at dinnertime at the table like the Waltons, but Dad you taught me the world and how to work it. I knew how to drive a forklift before my peers knew how to tie their shoes. Thank you, Dad, because I still feel the same way here in prison. I see inmates who are not well-rounded and that's a waste.

But back to the weather. I knew when the chill was in the air the future was lonely to me—the same way I felt about the last eight years of my case. I couldn't make plans because my future was uncertain. I would have to leave. Well, this year Dad you left me to be with the Lord. That's the only way you would ever leave me. Now, for the first time in my life, I know that I'm on my own when the weather is changing. It's like when the bully tells you that he's going to beat you up at 3 p.m. Well, heck, I have to go home. I can't stay in school forever. So I tie my boots up tight and put on my chinstrap and go give it my all. I have no choice.

That's where I'm at now.

So as I write you this letter, I pause to put on a sweatshirt. I will now wear the warmth of Jesus in my body and the "you got to go home" courage as my persona, and trust that as we used to say in the NBA, "This is my season!"

I miss you, Big Fella!

Love,

J

Oxymoron

There is nothing that so much gratifies
an ill tongue as when it finds an angry heart.
~ Thomas Fuller

I do not touch the TV here in the public area of our prison tier. As I have seen and learned over the past seven months in here, the television gives, or should I say *adds* more time to your sentence than any other prison folly. But last night was an exception. I wanted to rip the television out of the wall and take the other 37 inmates back to the radio days. Let me explain. But first, I need to take a five-minute break to pray and meditate on this…

Okay, I'm civilized again. Kent, a 40-year-old devout Philadelphia Eagles fan, stood up in front of the television and announced that he is now a Houston Oilers fan, citing Mike Vick as his reason for switching.

"Michael Vick is a criminal and a low-life ***-hole that shouldn't even be in the NFL." Kent is white and a former sergeant on the NJ police department. I only mention he's white because Kent is also a self-proclaimed racist. Being a racist and on the police force should be an oxymoron, but then again, so should the rest of this observation.

First, how can Kent call Michael Vick a criminal? Isn't Kent on my tier right here at Mid-State Correctional Facility? And what did he do to become a convicted felon? Well, I'm glad you asked. Kent killed his wife, Michelle. Yes, he shot her, then stabbed her, then dismembered her body, and oh yeah, threw her remains in a wood chipper. And one more time—this is a decorated police sergeant. I could continue to explain everything that is wrong with this scenario, but it's too self-explanatory. Mike Vick repented. I know this because we go to the same church. He has taken responsibility for his actions and has paid his debt to society. Has Kent done the same? Hardly.

I wanted to get that out of the way because segueing back might be difficult after I share what I read in my morning devotional.

Proverbs 12:18 says, *"There is one who speaks like the piercings of a sword, but the tongue of the wise promotes health."* Our tongues can be like a multi-bladed Swiss army knife when it comes to the many ways that we cut and destroy each other. I read that unhealthy attitudes of anger, irritation, frustration and impatience—even hypocrisy, stress, guilt, and insecurity—all contribute to our damaging speech. We cut with our words. Personally, I know that when my attitude is unhealthy, my speech tends to be unhealthy, also. Basically, I need to watch what I say and deal with the way I feel. Time to put away the knife and use our words to help and heal others and ourselves.

And I will let the TV live.

Tantrums

Throw away thy rod, throw away thy wrath;
O my God, take the gentle path.
~ George Herbert, "Discipline"

Dear Dad,

I know you had a front row seat view to another one of my tantrums. Believe it or not, I think you are going to be privy to most of them because of the new hours I keep. See, jail lights go off at 10 p.m. and that's when the police leave and if you have a "beef," this is when you express yourself. I know you usually fall asleep in Heaven around 10:30 p.m., and believe you me, I try to wait until 10:45 p.m. to file my grievances. I like to give you my version at 6 a.m.; the truth is too simple, so I must always get there by a complicated route.

A few days ago I held a meeting with 37 other inmates and we voted on smoking at the back window of the tier only. As I've come to learn, we men have the attention span of a slice of bologna. I continually growl all day long, so by night I'm dog-tired.

"Raven" is a large, light-skinned black man who considers himself a master chameleon because he thinks he can also pass as a white man (but that's a whole other letter). I would love to drop him off at a KKK meeting and see how Caucasian he feels then. Anyway, Raven has a routine of borrowing Matt's Walkman every night and on this particular night, believe it or not, Matt lent his Walkman (yes, Dad, *his* Walkman—you see where I'm going with this?) to someone else. This made Mr. Selfish jealous and then here comes the tantrum. "He is a Nigga', yo!" and, "This is prison, yo!" and he let us all know that he will smoke "where and when he wants!"

Well, Dad, you always told me a jealous man always finds more than he is looking for. As ye smoke, so shall ye reek.

Well, reek this...

I explained to this racially confused con artist (in his ear so he wouldn't be embarrassed in front of the audience) that smoking was only allowed at the agreed-upon location. Raven then explained to me that, "We live in the Ghetto," and "He is a Nigga' and he will..."

He didn't have to finish because I interrupted him with these words, "If you don't get your confused behind off your bunk and go to that window with that cancer stick, I'm gonna snatch you off your bunk, turn you upside down, and shake the matches right out of your pocket!"

Dad, I didn't ask for this job of "Jayson can make everything right," and you know I'm not talking about prison only. I play the candle on both sides of the wall and I am not only consuming myself, but my wick is becoming a wretch! I must tread lightly, Daddy, otherwise the "No Vacancy" sign above my bunk will be glowing long after my release date comes and goes. Then I'm still here with the ravens, away from your granddaughters and everyone I love, and all because of a tantrum.

Benjamin Franklin said, "Remember not only to say the right thing in the right place, but far more difficult still, to leave unsaid the wrong thing at the tempting moment." Best way, Dad, is to go to the Bible because, inevitably, each one of us at times will be tempted to lash out in anger. Through God's work in our lives, we can learn to control our anger. What better way to influence people than through a gentle spirit?

Oh yeah, hold on, Dad.

"Raven," I whisper. "You can come away from the window now," I say tenderly, because he's been scared to move away for 13 hours.

Love you, Daddy,
Jayson

No Explanations

Dear Daddy,

Around 11 a.m. yesterday another inmate told me I had to go to the gate. He said that Earl was going nuts. Earl is a massive human being who works out constantly. When Matt and I were on our "Save The World" campaign, we planned to hook him up with a job as a professional trainer after his release in 16 months. I headed to the gate, upset because I thought they needed me to break up a fight or listen to a complaint. The latter is an understatement.

Earl was hysterical, sobbing uncontrollably. Daddy, that is a no-no in prison. Only one emotion will help you survive in here and that's anger. Before I could figure out what was going on, Earl ran into my arms and hugged me for five minutes as he kept screaming, "They executed my brother!"

Daddy, they shot him in the back of the head as he tried to escape the gang life. While he laid there begging for another chance, they shot him again in the head.

If crying is a no-no here in prison, then crying while hugging another inmate is a definite, *Heavens, no!* At least that's what I thought, anyway. Not true. You know I'm a hugger and if I could hug every morning I would.

See, Dad, I know what it's like to have a sibling shot to death. Your daughter, Ann, was shot in the face by her coward of a husband. God spares me no painful experiences in my life. None! There was no theory on how to handle Earl, just experience. There is nothing you should do in this situation but hug as hard as you are being hugged. Silence on my part is the best anesthesia. Dad, I felt terrible. So sad. No words can comfort another man who can't get to his family because of his own past convictions. This was new to me. I knew I couldn't get in a vehicle and drive him to more familiar arms to hug him. This is terrible. It sucks! You are built like Tarzan, but as helpless as Jane.

Prison will allow you or should I say *guarantee* you isolation, as much as you desire. But not for Earl. He told the corrections officer he didn't want to be alone, that he was fine right there with me. Dad, do you know what the saddest thing of all is? And excuse me for using the word "sad" over and over, but it's the simplest and most effective adjective. The saddest thing was that Earl just met me and I'm the only person he had to hug.

God, please, I beg You! Don't keep me in here so long that I lose someone I should have hugged more as a free sinner. But God, sometimes you make my life—no, You *allow* my life to be more complicated than a tiger's eye. You won't grant me this mercy, will You God? That's why You gave me such strong shoulders. That's why You gave me this isolation—to make these shoulders even stronger. No problem, God. I have to "let go and let You."

There are 37 other inmates in here, Dad, and God directed instant pain to just two: one, because he is the brother and the other, because "Jayson" means "healer" in the Bible. I can't end this letter without explaining myself a little bit more.

Dad, if my pen breathes agitation, this pen hasn't lied yet today. I have seen and caused more pain than

No Explanations

anyone I have encountered, by far. God has once again reminded me that I can't hide. He, for His own reasons, will not allow me to become robotic. I, like Jonah, have journeyed from Him. I have even sided with the Dark Side temporarily because I believed one man shouldn't have to endure so much.

Why, Dad, did He let you lie there with bedsores that all the money He gave me couldn't prevent? You were my best friend and not only did He paralyze your limbs, but He took your strongest muscle (especially for me)—your tongue.

Dad, I know you now have a physical relationship with Him because you are sitting right next to Him and you can hug Him. But I'm upset every time He tries to make things right with me. And yes, I do think about the fame and fortune! And yes! I will give it back to Him every time! That's why I gave so much money away, Dad! But when I think about it, I can't even get even with Him because I'm still just fitting right into His master plan. I'm helping someone else, thus, He wins.

I won't ride with the Dark Side, either, but man, why keep giving me such pain? Why let you lay there for two years helpless? Why take three sisters? Why let Linda die at 41 pounds? Why? He built me. He knows I don't like bullies.

The best way to learn about a product is to ask the inventor, so Dad, I will keep asking Him.

Since I was 13 1/2 years old, You have shown me such pain, Dude! I never complained, heck, I just did what needed to be done. Instinctively. You had me taking care of people when I should have been in Little League. I can go on with this letter for an endless amount of time. But Dad, I'm upset with Him and before I disrespect the two people who love me the most, I will end this letter in the same manner God ended it with me.

No explanations!...

Like a Child

"When I was a child, I spoke as a child, I understood as a child, I thought as a child; but when I became a man, I put away childish things."
I Corinthians 13:11

Dear Big Daddy,

Today you would have been proud of me. Let me once again set the stage. I had two childhood friends come and visit me. After the visit we must line up and be humiliated for the safety of the CO's and for our own safety. Just this procedure alone will make you contemplate a visit that may be sub par. But since I must stop acting like a child and being selfish, I quickly reminded myself how uncomfortable it is for the innocent civilians who visit and have to be searched and humiliated.

When I first came to prison, I asked a fellow inmate a silly question. Sydney is a very large man with 17 years in. "Sydney, why do you walk on egg shells here? It seems you are in control." Sydney became instantly angry and didn't hold back even though I was wet behind the ears and a high-profile individual. He shouted, "Control! How in the hell can I be in control when another man can just decide he is having a bad day and make me

Like A Child

drop my pants and look up the crack of my backside?" As I tried to agree with him, he, in so many words (as a matter of fact, no words) just pointed me out of his cell.

So back to my situation. After my visit, I had a 20-something year-old CO named Gelder search me. Just because Gelder works here doesn't make him immune to immaturity. He is a wannabe marine, I'm guessing, because of the shine on his boots and jug head haircut, along with an unnecessary loud and demanding tone of voice.

Anyway, Gelder tried to humiliate me by keeping me naked for an extraordinary amount of time while he made me turn my underwear inside out more than a few times, when this is not procedure. As I continued to oblige each time he barked out his unauthorized orders, he became even angrier. Dad, let me explain some of this "child's" antics. First, he needed to be the center of attention in front of the other CO's. "I humiliated Jayson Williams! Just wait until I go home and tell my other idiot friends (who probably condone this type of behavior) tonight over a Budweiser!" Second, Officer Gelder was insensitive to my feelings. Thirdly, children don't have the ability to look ahead.

Now, I could have acted like a five-year-old, also, and thrown a temper tantrum. But unlike a child, I'm not naive. I noticed the dismay on his Commanding Officer's face, so I did as I was told and headed back to my cell knowing an apology was probably coming from the Lieutenant. I have been an ideal prisoner and unlike a child, I have been consistently respectful. Most of all—unlike the child who tried to humiliate me—I displayed will power.

The Lieutenant came over and said, "Williams, I apologize. You give these kids some authority and they abuse it. I saw the whole thing and CO Gelder was 100% out of line and he will be disciplined for these immature actions." I agreed with him and said, "All kids are irresponsible and unprofessional at times."

The Lieutenant then reprimanded CO Gelder in front of other officers, the Inmate Liaison Committee (ILC) Chairman, and me. As the Lieutenant walked away, the ILC Chairman, Karroway, stuck out his chest and proudly said, "The CO was wrong, you didn't have to say thank you." To which I responded, "Only children are unappreciative."

Love you,
Jayson

New Jail Smell

Up, sluggard, and waste not life;
in the grave will be sleeping enough.
~ Anonymous

Dear Daddy,

My fellow inmate "K" and I have been scheming for over six months on how to smuggle some paint onto our prison tier. I thought a fresh coat of paint on the walls and footlockers might give everyone a self-esteem boost and if nothing else, we could spend a day or two watching paint dry.

Counting on the chaos and the DOC's weak chain of command, along with K and I acting like this is routine procedure happening all over the rest of the prison, we got right to work—K with his paintbrush and me with my toenail clippers to cut away the strings inmates use for clotheslines. We figured most would appreciate the fact that out of New Jersey's 25,000$^+$ prisoners, we were likely the only ones afforded this privilege.

Wrong!

We weren't asking for much at 2:30 p.m. on a slow Tuesday in prison, but in order for this covert operation to be successful, we needed the inmates to wake up and move out of our way. But this is prison, and it's never that easy.

One of the first to slow the operation was Holy Joe, a self-centered pedophile who likes to pretend he is never asleep, but always praying. "Patience is often mistaken for laziness," he says to me all godly-like, after I pointed out his slothfulness. "You have the devil of impatience on your shoulder, Mr. Williams, and she will take you straight to hell."

I just stood there at his bunk, unfazed, waiting for him to get out of bed so we could start the job. Patience has its limits in here, Daddy. Take it too far and people may think I'm a coward.

Holy Joe, raising his voice a little louder now so the rest of the lazy natives still lying in their bunks could hear, keeps going, "Yes, sir, Mr. Williams. That devil of impatience is a terrible thing, and she's gonna take you *rriiiight* to hell!"

Glaring down at him, I gripped the bunk with both hands and gave it a quick jerk. The rattle was enough to get the holy man to at least look up at me.

"That's right, Holy Joe, I have a devil on my shoulders," I shot back. "But at least mine is over 21 years of age. Now you get your lazy self off this bunk so I can paint it, or you won't have to worry about hell, cause I'm gonna knock it right out of you!"

Unbelievable.

Remember back on the farm, how I would give you the real scoop on your crew, which ones were working and which ones were slacking off? Well, more than half of the inmates resisted (pretty close to the current recidivism rate) and one inmate even went and snitched, complaining that the fumes were making him sick. I reminded the CO that this man is in prison because he's been inhaling crack cocaine and the issue was quickly resolved (and even rewarded) with a spontaneous belly laugh.

Thankfully, there were some who were able to recognize our paintbrush for what it was: a tool to improve their self-respect and community. They saw that we genuinely cared and they were happy to cooperate, and some even thanked us afterwards.

Oh yeah, my place now has the new jail smell. LOL.
Miss you,
Jayson

Let it Rain!

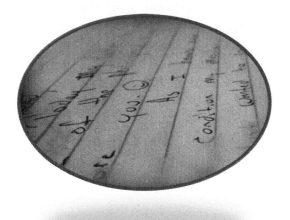

Dear Dad,

Today my letter to you will be one of a philosophical manner. I hope I don't bore you. As I headed out to the Big Yard to condition my muscles in the pouring rain, I just wanted to reminisce about the morning rains when I was nine years old riding under the Hudson River, hoping that when the tunnel released us into another state, the skies would be even more unforgiving than when we entered. This meant we would have the day off, because bricks could withstand Mother Nature, but not in their birth state.

I couldn't help but shake my head in agreement as I remembered what you used to tell me about the rain, and the men who won't work in it. I watch 50 inmates continue to press weights toward the composer of the liquids, not missing a beat, and think, *But if lifting*

Let It Rain!

weights was their job and it was raining, they would make more noise than an empty wagon. They would make a million excuses to call it quits. That is my recollection of when I was a child.

When I took short intermissions from God in my prime of sin, the rain was also a welcoming excuse. Being a winebibber at night and a "Type A" personality in the day, the rain provided the window illusion that I wasn't missing anything anyway so I could rest my aching head. Un-productivity was then the victor.

Now in prison, surrounded by grey bars, walls, and grey skies, the rain produces tranquility and undistracted time with God. My peers distinctly remember this as a time of no drug deals, murders, or crimes because of the chaos and confusion it caused on the streets. God forbid they should get damp while doing the work of the devil. Okay, Dad, that was my funny for the day because I know myself too well. When the ill mind is awake with sunshine on the brain, for want of being sufficiently disciplined by recollection, especially when first engaged in devotion, I sometimes give in to certain bad habits of wandering and dissipation. They are difficult to overcome and uncommonly draw me, even against my will, to the things of earth. I believe it is then that I should confess my faults and humble myself before God—short and sweet— without the multiplicity of words in prayer. When it rains in prison it's quiet so my will then brings my prayers back to tranquility. It's then my business to keep my mind in the presence of the Lord.

The word "rain" in the American Heritage College Dictionary means many things, one being "to force the cancellation or postponement of..." Most people (besides farmers, and now me, a prisoner) see this as despair. But the very next word in this dictionary is "rainbow," an illusory of hope. When the rain cancels the disquiet, I find it easy to keep my mind calm in a

time of prayer, or at least to recall it quickly from its wandering.
So let it rain!
Love,
Jayson

Help Wanted

*The most dangerous of all falsehoods
is the slightly distorted truth.*
~ G.C. Lichtenburg

Dear Dad,

The prison barber is one of the most dangerous jobs behind these walls. The *most* dangerous job is impersonating the prison barber. I just watched a 60-year-old Italian inmate called Paisan take the *Help Wanted* sign down and prepare his "shop" for clients. Paisan sleeps 80% of his sentence away, ("professional jailing") and because of his diabetes, he starts to go blind at the top of the hour. Now, why an old Italian diabetic would want to volunteer to cut an African-American gang leader's hair is beyond me, but it seems prisoner "Fu" will be the first unlucky recipient of Paisan's folly.

It's been a slow morning, so I grab my Bible and pull up a chair. Calamity is sure to follow, and I will be pretending to read while it happens, because they cannot call a witness who was preoccupied with reading.

"You took your medication, Italiano?" Fu cautiously asks.

I bury my head in the Book of Judges. Chapter 16 and Samson being betrayed by Delilah will be a nice backdrop for the dark opera, "The Barber of Seville," unfolding just a few feet away.

I peer over my Bible as the butchering begins. I can only laugh (in my head) because I keep picturing Alfalfa from the Little Rascals singing, "I'm the Barber of DeVille." But as soon as that childhood memory stops soothing me, I look up to find another. Paisan is busily circling Fu, the bottom half of Fu's head now completely bald. I keep picturing Richard Prior and his skit about Italians putting bowls on all the "brothas' heads," and then cutting around the edge to make them appear Chinese so they could get jobs working on the railroad. But my laughing stays behind my Bible, as Fu is beginning to question the roar of the clippers.

Daddy, it always amazes me how we inmates get offended when society labels us untrustworthy and useless, but we do the same thing to each other all the time. Fu was skeptical about Paisan's barber credentials right off the bat. I think Abraham Lincoln said it best, *If once you forfeit the confidence of your fellow [inmate], you can never regain their respect and esteem.*

Fu, like all of us in here, has selfish ambitions, including vanity, lack of trust, insecurity, and the token know-it-all mentality of every inmate I've ever met. Now, add to that a prison "shank" (weapon/knife) and one should pick his clients wisely. I would consider someone like myself to be a good candidate because my honesty has a little bit of Watergate mixed in. I would probably just say, "Fine job, Paisan." And then grab a broomstick and start brushing my head with it, praying that if I keep playing with it, it will eventually grow back.

Help Wanted

But back to the show.

By this point, Daddy, there is no need to watch anymore. Paisan just finished up singing his Frank Sinatra songs, and is well into his Howard Cosell play-by-play, explaining his every move like he's hosting some kind of cooking show, only for prison barbers.

Since inmates would only use mirrors for vanity, never to look for flaws, and after a botched lobotomy or two, someone was smart enough to get rid of all the glass in this prison. So one glance in the 6x8 reflective aluminum foil sticker was all it took for Fu to catch on.

I peer over the edge of my Bible to see Fu's face all twisted up as he leans forward in his chair. He's shifting from side to side and surveying the damage. He takes a long, deep breath and then exhales in a short burst of anger.

"Give me the clippers and I will finish it myself!!" Fu hisses.

"Nah, nah, Brotha'. Let it grow back in. I don't know what fool cut your hair last time, but he really screwed your head up." Paisan is back talking to his audience, looking right over Fu's head into his imaginary TV camera.

"The next time I cut your hair it will look better," Paisan reassures him, lovingly patting him on the shoulder before turning around to shake the hair from his clippers. He whistles a happy tune as Fu rises from his chair, squares up, and begins to rock up and down, heel to toe, fists balled, seething with rage. Paisan is still humming Frank Sinatra while brushing the hair from his prison khakis.

Without warning, Fu grabs Paisan's left shoulder and whips him around counter-clockwise. Now they have some eye contact. Paisan looks a little off balance, but is still humming his tune.

"You can't cut my hair again." Fu whispers angrily.

Paisan looks puzzled. "Why?"

Daddy, the scream that came from Fu's mouth was something like a dragon in labor. "BECAUSE I'M GONNA KILL YOU, THAT'S WHY!"

Show over, Daddy.

And when was it you said you were coming, again? You know, coming to take me home to New York City?

Miss you,
Jayson

Cobwebs & Cables

We are what we repeatedly do.
Excellence, then, is not an act, but a habit.
~ Aristotle

Dear Daddy,

After almost eight months in prison, I am starting to agree with Confucius: "The nature of man is always the same, but it's their habits that separate them." In prison, you can tell a bad habit right from Jump Street. I look at a career criminal, who in most cases is a drug addict, and I can't help but wonder about the sequence of events and choices that led to his customary behavior patterns.

His habits were first cobwebs, then cables. Sometimes my empathy turns to sympathy and I must become continuous, or productive and robotic, because sympathy can make me appear weak, and that can be fatal in this Closter land of dangerous habits.

But this day, I didn't have to go anywhere to get advice. It came to me by way of one of my most trusted new people in the second half of this vapor (life) of mine.

Karroway must have seen the bewilderment on my grill as I stared at two other inmates. Without even an "Excuse me," or "Are you busy right now?" Karroway pounced with a mouthful of explanations about bad habits.

"See this article? Read it. It's about people just like you and Matt who tried to help these prisoners make it on the other side of these walls and who get taken advantage of. It happens every time cuz some people are just too sick to be helped. They have what's called 'Dope Fiend Mentality', or 'D.M.' for short. Check it out. There are five characteristics and once you spot them, stand back. Avoid these fools at all costs because there is no saving them."

1. Inconsiderate
2. Strife—angry contention, a rivalry
3. Envy
4. Selfishness
5. Greed

Only two things can help them.
1. God, and that's self-explanatory
2. Identify and pen their issues

Karroway went on to explain that all these guys have suppressed issues from childhood. "If they don't deal with these issues, they won't get better. They are just enjoying three hots and a cot (prison) and wasting everyone's time. They sleep, eat, watch TV, and say to themselves, *Dang! I DID do something wrong. I got caught!* And then back to their procrastination they go!"

Just like that, Karroway gets up and leaves, like a judge who just slammed down the gavel and left the bench, disgusted that he even has to witness these types of cases in the first place.

I sometimes blame others, Daddy. *Nothing so needs*

reforming as other people's habits, I used to think. Isolation has made me fully cognitive of my own patterns. And the inmate in here who just helped me with this next quote happens to be a former carpenter, so I thought it fitting, Dad, to leave you with this quote from Desiderius Erasmus: "A nail is driven out by another nail; habit overcome by habit."

I will continue to deal with my habits. And since Jesus was also a carpenter and you are in His presence, please ask Him: Has He ever missed the nail and hit His thumb? LOL.

Had to do it, Daddy.

Love you Dad and Jesus,
Jayson

Can't Be Ruined

I don't know the key to success,
but the key to failure is trying to please everybody.
~ Bill Cosby

Dad,

Today I woke up totally discombobulated. I thought it was Sunday and my mind was racing with confusion all through our morning workout. I tried to explain myself to Matthew, but couldn't. The effort was there, but the conversation eventually died. Matthew kept nodding his head like, *C'mon. You gotta give me something to work with,* but I had nothing to give.

Today my ignorance cramped our conversation. Today I don't want to work for Jesus. Today I feel I'm not fit to, and my conversation mirrored my thoughts. *I'm not getting better in prison.* That was my first thought after I figured out it was Tuesday, not Sunday.

Last night I asked Matthew what he wanted to do when he gets out of prison and he didn't really know. Me neither. I told him that I hope to work with our youth someday, I hope to be used by God for His purpose, and I hope to save the world. Not today, though. On days like today, I feel ill equipped to do anything worthwhile.

I was talking to Matthew and accused his friend "Snap" of being a pedophile without any proof—just a gut feeling I had. And when I heard Snap say that he liked black females, I became instantly enraged and told him that he only took advantage of black girls because statistically, black fathers are not around. Dad, *I'm not around for my kids.* I attacked a man's character based on a hunch just to divert attention from my own wrongs. For that, Daddy, I'm ashamed. I will pull Snap to the side and apologize.

Something has not been right with me lately. I don't trust myself and as they say, he who mistrusts most, should be trusted least. It is equally wrong to trust all men or no man. I'm becoming institutionalized. I'm starting to think the judicial system is right and I'm a bad person. I fear I'm using the system as a crutch to hide from society. I don't think I can be who they want me to be on the other side of these walls.

There are people around me who hurt children, and someone asked me a hypothetical question about whether or not I would ever "go out and have a beer with a pedophile" upon my release. I said I would, but that I wouldn't leave them alone with my children. Okay, let me go back and underline "my children." That's selfish! What, it's "okay" as long as they are not hurting people I love? On the other hand, should I be harder on the pedophiles because I was selfish enough to come to prison and am not there to protect my children? Or am I fooling myself into thinking that being harder on the pedophiles is sufficient enough to make it good with my daughters? This is the garbage I'm pumping to myself. What is wrong with me?

Matthew explained that because this is prison, I must realize that I'm just associating with people who do premeditated bad things because there is nowhere else to go. Daddy, I help the pedophiles more than anyone else in here. I just said I would have a beer with them upon my release. Okay, but am I trying to help these people or just pat myself on the back to deflect attention? I do feel soft because I don't tell them to repent like I did. My conscience makes a coward of me over and over.

This issue is about me, not pedophiles. If you had asked me last week if I was ready to make a change for God, or do God's work, I would have said, "Almost. I'm getting there." But not today. I've been in prison for almost eight months and today, I want to be released from prison or not. I don't want the pressure of being someone who can make a change. Since I'm in prison around "bad people" or "simple people," as my ex-wife put it, I thought people would no longer put me under a microscope. Not that for a minute I don't realize my status in society, but I just wanted to let my guard down for once. But Holy Joe won't allow it.

Dad, writing these letters to figure out "Am I who they say I am?" has helped me so much because when I first started writing this letter to you, I was totally confused. Now I'm figuring it out. Or are *we* figuring it out? Or am I just plain making excuses and deflecting attention on others?

God, You made me special for Your purpose. I can't just flip the switch of clarity whenever I feel game. I must steadily focus on Your purpose, and then my purpose will become evident. Focus! I must focus!

I can now answer the question I posed to Matthew last night. I want to be content. That's what I want now *and* when I get out. If I can become content, I <u>can't</u> be ruined. A contented mind is a continual feast, Dad, and the best of blessings is a contented mind.

Dad, these pedophiles can't hurt my daughters while they are locked up. I just wanted to take a break from focusing on me and getting better. I have never run from a fight so why start now? Especially since I'm fighting the carelessness and recklessness of Jayson. The only tyrant I accept in this prison is still the voice within.

Holy Joe has to fight his own battles, not judge mine. We can sharpen one another, but not at the folly or expense of others. I can't worry about changing or judging others at this fragile time in my recovery. I must stop being impatient and fooling myself by telling God to "Put me in the game now or else You will lose me for a season!" Impatience and malcontent have no room in the Williams' men's hearts. Am I right, Dad? I will continue to have a good heart and tell these guys what Jesus has done for me and leave it at that. Jesus will do the rest!

Love you, Daddy!
Jayson

Lessons at Eight

Good Morning, Dad,

I should have started this letter to you at 4:40 a.m., but the lighting was insufficient. Even at 4:40 a.m. I heard a *tack, tack, tack, tack* every minute or so for 15 minutes. Since it's October, I'm thinking this must be the first time the heat has arrived via the pipes in the bathroom. No, couldn't have been. The rhythm was too pompous. Yes, pompous.

So I went to investigate, only to find Paisan shaving. Remember this character, Dad? A 60-year-old Italian man who sets the Italians back...well, I was going to say 400 years, kind of like Mr. T did for our race. Believe it or not, Paisan still talks like this, "Aeeeee...ooohh, what'sa matta', you?" I could see if he just arrived off the boat, but he's been in prison for 10 years and he's from Philadelphia!

Dad, when I addressed him about his selfishness, he replied, "Well, you laugh and joke around when I'm sleeping." I'm thinking, *Paisan, it's noon when you're sleeping! You sleep 20 hours a day, man!* He has one thing going for him though. He is much older than I am so I can't "tighten him up."

Okay Dad, let's get to work on improving me now.

Dad, all I really need to know about how to live this life I learned before I was eight years old:

> There is only one God.
> Don't listen to strangers.
> Don't curse and call people
> ugly names (make fun).
> Go to church on Sundays and
> say your prayers every night.
> You and Mom are the bosses.
> Don't hurt anyone.
> Don't cheat and always play fair.
> Share everything.
> Don't take something that
> doesn't belong to me.
> Don't tell fibs.
> Clean up after myself.
> Every living creature dies and
> goes to be with God if they're good
> and love God.
> Take a bath at least every two days. (LOL)
> And it is still true, no matter how old you are
> when you go out into the world,
> it is best to hold hands and stick together.

I've noticed that most of these have held true over the years and still apply today. Just think what a beautiful life I would have had if I had stayed true to God's Ten Commandments, and Mom's and yours. Well, Dad, it's a part of growing up and it's never too late to grow up.

Oh, yeah, I forgot the part about having milk and

cookies, and a nap at 3 o'clock. But don't worry, the Department of Corrections is supplying me with those now.

Love you, Big Daddy,
JW

In A Puddle

Dear Daddy,

Yes, I became nervous and filled with anxiety for the first time in prison. I lost my peace of mind. Almost halfway before my parole date I lost my mind. I just made a phone call to confirm the letter I received from Michael Rowe, the former boss of the NJ Nets. He kept his promise about setting me back up as soon as I got halfway to the other side of these walls. But I'm not sure I was ready for this yet. I've been ducking him for weeks now, but he knows me better than I think he does. He called my manager, Akhtar, and gave him a piece of his mind, reminding him that he gave me 86 million dollars and it's time to get back in the swing of things. No excuses. "Tell Jayson to stop hiding. The world awaits!" Michael Rowe yelled.

Friday we had 8:00 a.m. recreation and not only did I try to find ways to hide from Mr. Rowe, I made excuses not to speak to Jesus about this. I went outside and was too unfocused to lift weights for long. I headed over to the court bench and quickly fell asleep in 55-degree raining weather to everyone's amusement, because they all headed for shelter closer to the prison.

I had a dream that I was trying to teach middle

school students from a book I had written. I was substituting for former NBA player Rob Phelps, current Dean of Students who teaches in NYC who couldn't be there. I couldn't find anything I needed. I remember thinking that the book I was holding wasn't right for 8th graders, but I opened it in front of the class and hoped for one manageable story. I couldn't find one and became even more frustrated. But I heard somebody telling me to read it the way it says on the page. Not knowing what the story contained or what it was even about, I winged it.

"Your only unforgivable mistake is the one you won't acknowledge. Your children know you're not flawless and they can handle it. They also know how big you have to be to admit it, and they're quick to forgive. So forget modeling perfection because we are far from perfect: just show them with a humble heart and teach them constructively how to handle it when they've been imperfect. We must be their examples and the accountability starts with you and me."

And I know I'm dreaming, not only because I'm reciting the words from our morning devotional from *The Word for You Today,* and not my book, but also because I feel the rain and wind hitting my face. Using the weather as an excuse to escape, I woke myself all the way up and then instantly jumped to my feet. But I didn't know my legs were asleep and did a sideways somersault right over the bench and onto my back.

Now I was fully awake.

Half the prison yard is standing over me asking me if I'm okay. Embarrassed, I laughed, "Yeah, I'm just doing an abdominal stretch."

"In the middle of a puddle?" an inmate asked.

Dad, Jesus has dealt with me privately and publically before, and today He is dealing with me in public once again. I immediately listened this time and went back to my cell to pray and get some clarity. I became the pre-

In A Puddle

prison Jayson again, restless and filled with fear and anxiety. It's a truly terrible feeling in prison because you have no one. I prayed but I just felt helpless. After a few phone calls to cancel my weekend visits and trying to give instructions to people who didn't understand my sense of urgency because my release date is still a pregnancy away, I went back to my bunk to read and analyze the situation. I came up with a few short-term solutions to temporarily ease my mind.

I can't try to change people in my life. Only God can change them. I try to make things happen when it's not the right time and just like a child, I've again become impatient. God wants and needs me to grow out of this. I usually get upset and flustered because I'm not progressing fast enough. I must learn to be content with where I am and let Jesus handle my worries. "Be Still!" I keep pushing myself harder and harder. I do what I *think* God wants without even checking with Him about what He actually wants, when He wants it, or how He wants it done. I wear myself out. God knows my heart and that I feel I only have one more chance at this. But God is not the God of a second chance. My God is the God of *another* chance. God gives perfect peace to those who keep His purpose firm and trust in Him.

For now, I'm trying to work on getting healthy. And this time I promise not to run— or should I say fall right on my back.

Love you.
Jayson

Just Do Me

"O, it is excellent to have a giant's strength,
but it is tyrannous to use it like a giant."
~ Shakespeare

Dear Daddy,

All month I have felt the presence of the "other side." If I'm not careful, *very* careful, I can appease that side temporarily again. Or close to it. I know my limitations. I'm surrounded by sinners like myself, but the difference is I am remorseful. In prison you can't choose who they place you with, but you can choose who you walk with. If I always walk with the lame, I myself will learn to limp.

The people who agitate my soul must be devils, especially to harm the innocence of God's greatest gift, children. Dad, the confession of evil works is the first beginning of good works. If they are too embarrassed to confess to God—or do you think they don't believe they were completely 100% wrong? Nothing spoils a confession like repentance. Not to me, to God. Then I will take their new actions, observe them, pray on it, and move cautiously in their presence.

Today is October 31st, Halloween, and I almost had to play Jason! Nine months in prison and I fell right back into the same s***. Bad company! Yes, Dad, in prison church, of all places. Red Rum, a leader of one of the notorious gangs, was sitting behind me at the halfway point in the gym where we hold our service. Of all things, he and four of his soldiers held a two-hour conversation about killing a snitch here at Mid-State. Yes, Dad, of course the alleged snitch is in my circle. I will write you later in the week about that one. Wow.

Red Rum and his a**** were conspiring so loud that we couldn't concentrate on the preacher's message. The congregation didn't want to address these gangbangers so they turned on a 45-degree angle, just enough to make my eye contact. See, I'm everybody's teddy bear until I must be their Grizzly, also.

I get a lot of heat because of my association with a bunch of grown black men (mostly) who go to Jumu'ah every Friday at noon. Jumu'ah is a celebration for Muslims, like a church service for Christians. But Muslims get "prayed up" and don't leave their prayers at the door like we Christians do. They put it into the physical. No gang member, priest, or 'god' would dare hold a conversation while the khutbah (testimony) was going on. To put it like the imam (Muslim speaker) said Friday, "Any Muslim who will disrespect Islam by being a pedophile should first be thrown off the highest mountain, then half their head cut off." I've noticed that Muslims stick together like we Christians are supposed to do. Remember Ecclesiastes 4:12, *"A threefold chord is not quickly broken."* But my congregation doesn't need unity—they have me, the self-proclaimed best a** kicker. The best that ever did it. The best in the world. Bull****, man! Dad, why am I cursing? I never curse in front of you. But as I'm writing this letter I've been interrupted at least a dozen times. From questions about Winnie the

Pooh, to when did Michael Jackson first moonwalk, to "Let me read the book Miguel showed you." (The name of the book is *I Hope They Sell Beer in Hell*.)

I only have a Bible in front of me with earplugs in. See the devil sends his friends right after church or fellowship. Trust me, Dad.

Anyway, I play basketball with Red Rum and some of his jacka*****. So Jayson being Jayson and not wanting to embarrass the "gang" and then them feeling some kind of way about me, I sold out. But check this out, Dad. If these dudes were talking about me, I would've picked them up, turned them upside down, and shaken those silly bandanas off their heads. Instantly I would've addressed them if they offended me. But not God?

"Just do me," a saying a selfish person uses when it benefits them not to get involved for selfish reasons. What's the difference, Dad? I don't do what the Bible says when it talks about bad company. 1 Corinthians 5:9, *"I wrote to you in my epistle not to keep company with sexually immoral people."* I probably will use the Jayson Williams "cover-up," and take verse 10 out of context, *Yet, I certainly did not mean with the sexually immoral people of this world, or with the covetous, or extortionists, or idolaters, since then you would need to go out of the world.*

I'm guilty of sexual immorality, Daddy, but not against anyone's will or any children. I was a freak—inherited probably from Mom. *Right*. But that's another letter. You and I can blame our infidelities on Mother. LOL.

Christians like me are called to influence the world, not run away and put my head in the sand like an ostrich; I think I'm hiding but my rear is sticking out for the world to see. I'm not running for president of the USA. I can't play politics with Jesus. Do as the Bible says all the time, not when it fits my conveniences.

But Dad, I do have good news. I am learning here in

Just Do Me

isolation. I waited until after the jailhouse preacher finished his lilywhite unprepared sermon that made whoever was talking fall asleep, and turned around to Red Rum and the Little Rascals. I whispered to them in a Clint Eastwood "Make My Day" tone, "Meet me tomorrow in the Big Yard at 1pm. What you guys did here is unacceptable," as all my fellow "Peters" looked on, happy that the Grizzly had once again roared to their defense. But if I had to fight these gang members, they would have denied me four times before I got stabbed once.

See, Dad, I was upset so I took time to pray and calm down and come up with a smart plan of action. If the old Jayson was here he would have beaten up "the gang that can't shoot straight" and then expect a tickertape parade. But guess what? The church would be no more and I probably would have added two more years away from your grandchildren.

Because of the way I carry myself in prison, not beating my drum too often to look like a hothead or a man with a feeble swagger, Red Rum apologized to me before I left prison church. Not wanting to be involved with him for another reason I discovered when I was "ear hustling" their conversation about killing my friend, the snitch, I just said, "I'm not the man you have to get right with. Jesus is that dude."

Now, Dad, I can "Just do me."

Love you, Dad,
Jayson

Self

Dear Daddy,

In prison, a man has no personality. He is a minor disposal problem and a few entries on reports. Nobody cares who loves or hates him, what he looks like, or what he did with his life. Nobody reacts to him unless he gives them trouble. Nobody abuses him. All that is asked of him is that he goes quietly to the right cell and remains quiet when he gets there. There is nothing to fight against, nothing to be mad at. The jailers are quiet men without animosity or cruelty. All this stuff you read about men yelling and screaming, beating against bars, running spoons along them, guards rushing in with clubs...all that is for the "Big House."

A fellow inmate, Rios, describes it this way: "A 'good' prison is one of the quietest places in the world. Life in jail is in suspension."

Dad, the walls and bars are strong and each day is like a year. I toss and turn in my cell like a roach that doesn't know where to die. I was taken and put into prison in handcuffs; it's not dominating, though I'm overwhelmed. I now understand my prison. My prison and enemy has been one and the same— SELF! I have been serving a 20-year sentence in the darkness of self.

I was riding in Rolls-Royces, private jets, and living in mansions. In the meantime, I was so incredibly and painfully sad and lonely. A pedestal is as much a prison as any small confined space. *Jayson Williams, NBA All-Star!* What a heavy burden is a name that has become too famous. Mark Wahlberg once told me the final test of fame is to have a crazy person imagine he is you. I wondered how someone could imagine being me when I don't even know me. Dad, life was moving too fast for this kid, your kid, Daddy.

When my mind went dormant, a part of my soul followed. My mind let my soul be reckless. I could always trick or bargain with my mind, but my soul had integrity. Mark 8:36 says, *"For what shall it profit a man, if he shall gain the whole world, and lose his own soul?"* Dad, you taught me correctly. I always knew when I was manipulating my soul.

Whenever I was getting ready to reason with my mind, I spent one third of my time making excuses to my mind and deciding what I was going to say to it, and two thirds thinking about my soul and what my soul was going to say to me.

Daddy, I am taking this prison isolation to reconnect with self. The pedestal of fame cannot be a light switch for me to use at my convenience. Fame should be instilled in me at all times for God's purpose. I cannot worry about the inmates who don't want to address their darkness. The only condition these sentences demonstratively cure is heterosexuality.

Dad, you and I used to watch the TV series *The Six Million Dollar Man*, the opening introduction claiming, "We can rebuild him (Steve Austin)...better than he was before. Better, stronger, faster." Isolation on a torn muscle rebuilds it. Isolation here in prison is rebuilding my mind, which in effect, won't tempt my soul. Dad, you couldn't help me with something you didn't notice. I'm an athlete and trained not to show any weakness or confusion. I'm now just a man minus the athlete in prison. There is nothing now that my body suffers that my soul does not profit by.

Get ready Dad, the second half is starting soon. This is the right place, the right time, and the right team.

Remember George Bush, the guy you voted for? (LOL) He said, "America is the land of the second chance—and when the gates of the prison open, the path ahead should lead to a better life." Our prison is self and the gate is now open! Let's keep it that way?

Love you, Big Man,
Jay

P.S. Did you vote today?

Down the Ladder

Dear Dad,

Just some biblical food for thought from my Bible study notes.

Most mornings, not every morning, the sun rose in splendor, but set in a tragic night. The downgrade of my life is the old familiar story of pride, egotism, and the presence of bad company. This led to moral degradation and ruin. Here are my steps down the ladder:

I was a good Christian boy (altar boy). My parents taught me at an early age to be humble and practice self-control. They circumcised me, taught me God's laws, and my Daddy taught me a trade.

I became wealthy and famous and independent of my father's ways.

I became disobedient and was guilty of rash vows.

Emptiness of God's purpose for me led me to envy,

false gods—sex, stimulants, alcohol, and folly.

I patronized the superstitions I had forbidden!

I put my faith in a medium and lawyers, not God.

I was wounded in a contest, and ended up in social suicide.

Having already destroyed my moral life, I ultimately destroyed my physical life (prison) and family's life.

Believe this Daddy, this sad story can still be repeated almost daily if I don't take heed!

Love,
Jayson

Egotistical, but True...

Chris Rock, the comedian, and I have been friends for over 20 years now. Right after my accident, when I became fair game to Jay Leno and my friend David Letterman, I went over to Chris' house and thanked him for not telling any jokes about me in his new movie. With a straight face he said, "Jay, only people on the East Coast know who you are."

So just to prove Chris Rock wrong, I picked up the phone and called Barbara Walters and met up with her for an exclusive one-hour national interview about my accident. Egotistical, but true. I also needed the jurors in my trial to hear my side of the story—just being honest.

Yesterday I received another year added onto my sentence for my DWI. I've been getting a lot of flack from the other prisoners. But I'm at peace with slander now. Slander slays three persons: the speaker, the spoken to, and the spoken of. I am satisfied knowing that God has more work to do on me, and He's given me more time to get healthy and complete my self-help programs. My freedom was once misguided happiness. People always ask me how it feels to lose my freedom. I reply, "How can I lose something I never had?"

God gave me another year here for my reckless choice, and only when He's finished with me will the whale spit me out on shore. I'm guilty! And this is a world of my own making.

Courage

Courage is not the absence of fear,
but rather the judgment that something else is more
important than fear.
~Ambrose Redmoon

Dear Mom,

In prison, the weaker and smaller inmates immediately become targets. Experienced prisoners try to study their M.O. and get what they can from the weak before they learn the system. Today—well, all week actually—has been quite interesting. I was part of an operation that stopped three homosexual prisoners from extorting one of our new inmates, who happens to be former law enforcement. These three losers assumed that this new inmate had gay tendencies so they brought a "trick" in his presence and claimed he took the bait. Then they filed a civil suit against the man and the DOC for emotional distress. Laughable and medieval! I thank God my word still carried some weight among "the powers that be" and we were able to pull off a sting. One of the three prisoners charged has 20 years in and a couple of stabbings, and another is a former corrections officer incarcerated for planting cocaine in an inmate's cell where he worked. Two out of the three were moved to another part of the prison, but the *head still remains.*

Mom, do you remember when you killed your first rattlesnake in South Carolina in 1974 when I was six? The kick from the shotgun knocked you down, but you shot that snake in half. When you went to pick it up, Granddaddy yelled at the top of his lungs, "Don't touch that snake! Even if you cut a rattlesnake's head off, it can still bite you up to an hour later and kill you." That image of a snake's head killing me made me sleep in your bed until I was 15. Of course, watching the movie *The Exorcist* around the same time didn't help. LOL.

Mom, you were so courageous.

Today I'm teaching about the 10 lepers Jesus healed (Luke 17:14-16). When I broke down the scripture, something hit home with me. In verse 14, Jesus reached out his hand and touched the man, not fearing the contagion of the disease. Mom, I'm scarred from the times when we went to visit Linda in the hospital in 1982. They treated her like a leper because AIDS scared the crap out of people 30 years ago. We even had to use the service elevator at Bellevue and her room was off-limits, blocked off like some sort of nuclear bomb factory. She looked so helpless lying there, her face deformed from being hit with a hammer several times and stabbed even more. They had her arms tied to the hospital bed with Ace bandages like she was a criminal. I totally understood it was because she would rip the I.V. tubes out. I knew Linda wanted out!

Mommy, there was even a sign on the door that all visitors were required to put on a non-contamination suit before entering. I refused to put on the "contagious outfit!" She was my sister! But, Mommy, you didn't refuse. What do you think Linda was thinking when she saw her mother there with a costume on before you greeted her? You weren't afraid of the rattlesnake, but you were cautious of your daughter's "contagiousness?"

I just wanted to scoop her up and take her out of there, and bring her back home with us where she belonged. Her room smelled like sickness and sadness and nobody wanted to talk about what we all feared the most. So we didn't. We just kept things light, and I tried to hug her a lot and kiss her, and make her feel like she was still home in our house with us. I grabbed her hands and I touched her face. I brushed her hair and told her that she was still the most beautiful person in the world to me. She needed to be with her family, not in that dungeon, or in the elevator reserved for trash and dead bodies. Oh yeah, Mom, it was me who used to cut the Ace bandages off her arms so she could move freely—a mystery that would always bewilder the hospital staff at Bellevue.

Well, Mom, I'm here in this tunnel I call a classroom, or "camp" as you describe it to your friends, and what the rest of my critics call "prison." And if I didn't write this to you and say all this, I wouldn't be able to let this scar go. I can now. Blood is blood. Don't be afraid of your own blood, Mom! I love you, Mommy. Enough said. Let's move on.

Why am I writing about this event and your courage right now? Today, Matt sent me a "kite" from another part of the prison where I used to be. His message said to beware of the new bald-headed guy who walks with a limp and answers to "Rocco." He's a plant, a stool pigeon, only there to set me up, snitch on me, and prevent me from making parole. He was another leper in the world's eyes. Too late! I already killed him. Relax, Mom, I killed him with the gentle genuine kindness you taught me! You taught me not to judge a person on reputation only, but also on character. So I fed him and showed him respect and he comes to our Bible study now. All this happened way before I received the warning from Matt.

Today at 5:45 a.m., while I was reading the story about the ten lepers, Rocco came over and politely interrupted and said with the most sincerity, "Thank you for helping me when no one would come near me!" Wow. Holy crap, Mom! Read this parable, Mom—the part about the one leper who thanked Jesus. Not only was that leper cured like the other nine, but because he came back and thanked Jesus, he now had salvation. Wow, Mommy.

I told Rocco about Jesus by my actions, by giving him food and showing him that he's not contagious. And now he attends the Bible study. So just maybe, Mom, by having courage in Jesus all the time, Rocco may be saved by the blood.

I love you, Mommy!
Jayson

VII.

The challenge of the believer is to take the faith that you got in here and take it to the place out there.
~ T.D. Jakes

Men & Boys
Save the World
Trouble Tree
Happy Thanksgiving
Up the Ladder
Super Mario
Hope
Cursing
Sleep Conversations
Let Sydney Sing
Rich or Poor
Merry Christmas
No Angel
Simple Solution
Shake it Off!
Take Heed
Do Over
Planted

Men & Boys

The Difference Between a Man and Boy
*Boys are students: Men are teachers
Boys are consumers: Men are producers
Boys play with toys: Men work with tools
Boys break things: Men make things
Boys ask questions: Men give answers
Boys are disruptive: Men bring order
Boys run in gangs: Men organize teams
Boys play house: Men build homes
Boys shack up: Men get married
Boys make babies: Men raise children
A boy won't raise his own children:
A man will raise his and somebody else's
Boys invent excuses for failure:
Men produce strategies for success
Boys look for somebody to take care of them:
Men look for somebody to take care of
Boys are present-centered; Men are time-balanced,
having knowledge of the past and understanding of the present and a vision for the future
Boys seek popularity: Men demand respect
Boys are up on the latest:
Men are down with the GREATEST.*
- Rev. Clarence L. James

Save the World

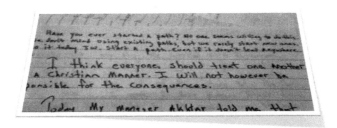

Have you ever started a path? No one seems willing to do this. We don't mind using existing paths, but we rarely start new ones. Do it today, JW. Start a path. Even if it doesn't lead anywhere.

Dear Daddy,

I think everyone should treat one another in a Christian manner. I will not, however, be responsible for the consequences.

Today my manager, Akhtar, told me that Rafi, the young man we helped get a hotel room for 30 days, clothing, and a job, called him very upset. "The job didn't come through," he said.

Now Matt and I tried to go through the state of New Jersey to set up a "Self-Imposed Progress" program, inmates helping inmates to help themselves. The state rejected it and we tried to do it anyway, which is difficult to do because we really have very little communication with the outside world. We thought that because we were professional athletes with influence and contacts, it would—at the very least—be the Christian thing to do.

Save The World

Or was it?

1. Akhtar's mom is in dire need of a kidney in the next few months or she shall die.
2. The only match is her son, my manager, Akhtar. Was that the Christian thing to do? Make him jump through hoops for someone he's never met?
3. Did I have any ulterior motives when we started this program? No, I didn't. I hope not.
4. Did I ask Matt to get involved just to lighten my load?
5. Well, I know it came from the heart. I was going to apologize to the other inmates on the unit for cursing up a storm once I heard that Louie didn't come though with the job he assured me "wouldn't be a problem." Louie is a former inmate who blew smoke. He worked at a furniture moving company and swore to me he could talk his boss into hiring Rafi. I purposely left Louie to the end of this story because he is not the problem. I am. I don't know Louie from a tealeaf. He might be a good guy, but he has his own problems being just recently released from prison. I have to realize that through my own recovered innocence we discern the innocence of our neighbors. Our intention was to help Rafi, no strings attached.

I'm upset at myself for two reasons:

1. Bothering my manager
2. Putting my "name" (brand) to something that failed. This one is very selfish of me. But my name is what I work so hard to preserve. Without that, even getting Rafi this far would have been more of a challenge.

The lesson from this whole mess? I must remember I'm in prison around prisoners. You always told me, "You can't get pee from a tree!" At least I'm not scared to try again. It is okay for my heart to be naive and for my mind not to be.

Enough said—lesson learned!

Love,
JW

Save The World

State of New Jersey
DEPARTMENT OF CORRECTIONS
WHITTLESEY ROAD
PO BOX 863
TRENTON NJ 08625-0863

CHRIS CHRISTIE
Governor

KIM GUADAGNO
Lt. Governor

GARY M. LANIGAN
Commissioner

June 23, 2010

Jayson Williams SBI 780161B
Mid-State Correctional Annex
PO Box 866
Wrightstown, New Jersey, 08562

Dear Mr. Williams:

Your letter to Governor Christie regarding your proposal for "Self-Imposed Progress (SIP)" was forwarded to my office for initial review. The Office of Transitional Services (OTS) offers standardized evidenced based best practice programming, within the correctional facility Social Services Department, designed to aid in reducing recidivism.

Thank you for your letter concerning improving the successful reentry for returning offenders. The Department appreciates the fact that "you completely understand your sentence and have taken full responsibility for your past actions". We applaud your desire to provide pre-release education to the offender population on the fundamentals of how to get and keep a job [section 1:B]. However, the Department currently offers two programs, SEALL and STARS, at each facility to address this issue. I have enclosed brochures of those programs for your perusal. Unfortunately, upon further review of your proposal, it lacks a detailed programmatic design and does not address the use of evidence based curricula.

Research has shown that educational achievement is the most paramount indicator in successful reentry. Considering your academic achievement, I suggest that you contact the Mid-state Education Department to offer your volunteer services as a tutor for those inmates in need of assistance with improving their literacy skills and/or achieving a GED. Thank you for your interest in reentry and best wishes with your endeavors.

Sincerely,

Darcella Sessoms, Director
Office of Transitional Services

Enclosures

c: G.O.C.R. (Workflow Id #1315479)
Lydell Sherrer, Assistant Commissioner (without brochures)
MSCA-Administrator's Office (without brochures)
Leila Morgan, Social Work Supervisor (without brochures)
Inmate Correspondence Unit Case # 10600032

New Jersey Is An Equal Opportunity Employer • Printed on Recycled and Recyclable Paper

Trouble Tree

*"Then you will lie down in peace and safety, unafraid; and I will bind you to me forever with chains of righteousness and justice and love and mercy.
I will betroth you to me in faithfulness and love and you will really know me then as you never have before."*
Hosea 2:14-20

Dear Dad,

One of the biggest tricks the enemy has ever played on me was convincing me that I would always have more time to spend with my family. *Go out with your friends! Keep working on that project, your family will be there when you get back.* Well, I never got that time back and when I finally made it home, my worldly troubles would consume our quality time there, also. That's because I always brought my troubles home with me. I tried to be everything to everybody. *A candle sheds light on others and consumes itself.* A true man takes care of his family first. I failed at this task more often than not. Why? Because I was selfish. What kind of Christian man would honestly display such behavior around people who love him?

I've been locked up for almost ten months now and I'm still approached by hundreds of people everyday. Since I was six years old, you've always taught me to treat everyone the way I would want to be treated. So here in prison, I continue to "play the candle," meeting and greeting them the way you and Mom taught me, with a smile and respect, even though I know that the majority are not Christians and don't have my best interest at heart. On the other side of the walls, you can regulate your company. It's not so easy here. It's a tough environment to give these people the benefit of the doubt, but I do as best as I can, and have learned a few things for the outside environment.

I can't try to please everyone and make them happy, except for my immediate family. I have to limit my quality time, including folly, charity events, and friends. Lastly, make a Trouble Tree. I do this here before I'm locked in for the night. Troubles won't help me in my cell or when I return to my family, so I just make believe I'm hanging my troubles on a tree limb in the Big Yard every night before I enter my cell. Then at 5:30 a.m., I pick them up again. A funny thing happens once I retrieve them, there aren't nearly as many as I remember hanging up the night before. Joy comes the night you hang your concerns up before you enter rest, and it always comes in the morning. (Psalm 30:5)

I can barely wait to put this theory to the test on the other side of these walls. I'm surrounded by people with one-liner clichés such as, *It's not quantity, it's quality time you spend with your family.* Once again, here in the World of Wrong, they are incorrect. I should spend all my quantity *and* quality time with my family. So now I finally have a family tree, Dad, even if it is the

Tree of Trouble.

Love you, Oak Tree!
Jayson (←Every family tree produces nuts—>Me!)

Happy Thanksgiving

Dear Daddy,

I remember the day before Thanksgiving being a hectic day for Mom. Between all the food shopping and phone calls, there was always the trip to Speedy's Tailor Shop. I was growing like a weed, and I only owned one suit at eight years old. Mommy being white and the tailor being Dominican, I could only piece together some of their conversations since I wasn't bilingual like Mom. But after letting out the tan nylon pants by two inches, the ones with the burgundy seam down the sides, we were off to Salvatore's barbershop on Mulberry Street in little Italy. Since I possessed Mommy's hair, I tended to always end up in barbershops like Salvatore's instead of Leroy's. Daddy, I think, or should I say, I *know* Salvatore tolerated this little black boy getting a haircut in his all-white barbershop on the busiest day of the year because he thought your wife was pretty. You still smiling, Dad? LOL!

Mommy to this day still talks about a particular time at Sal's. He was a loud and pretentious know-it-all Italiano, a "glass half empty" type of guy. When Frankie, one of his customers, said he'd be going to Rome on vacation and hoped to meet the Pope, Sal's reaction was his usual, "You?!" Sal mocked, "Meet the Pope? Don't make me laugh! The Pope only meets with important people. Why in the heck would he meet with you?"

A few weeks later, Frankie returned for another haircut. "How was Rome?" Sal asked him.

"Great! I saw the Pope!"

"From a distance with the rest of the crowd," said Sal.

"Yes, but then four guards came up, said the Pope wanted to meet me, and then they took me right up to his office in the Vatican."

"Get out of here, really?" Sal asked. "What did the Pope say?"

He said, "Who gave you that lousy haircut?"

Mommy loved telling that story, Daddy.

This day is our day, Dad. Let's be thankful for all the time God gave us together on earth. It's "but a vapor" compared to the eternity I will spend with you.

Happy Thanksgiving from Mom, Tryumph, and Whizdom!

Love you,
J

Up the Ladder

If a man is called to be a street sweeper, he should
sweep streets even as Michelangeo painted, or
Beethoven composed music, or Shakespeare wrote
poetry. He should sweep streets so well that all the
host of heaven and earth will pause to say, 'Here lived
a great street sweeper who did his job well.'
~ Martin Luther King, Jr., *The Strength to Love*

Dear Daddy,

Thank you! *For what*, you ask? For teaching me not one, but several trades. There's a young man named Blanco, yes "Blanco," because he's a Latin Kings gang member, but he's white. Blanco means white. Come on, Dad. Stick with me. I'm moving kind of fast. LOL! Blanco has been bounced from prison to prison four times in the last six years. That's very unusual, especially considering the fact that he's only 21 years old. He's 5'10 and weighs as much as a mosquito's backside. Quiet, but diabolical and sneaky. Or it might just be that he walks slow and squints because he's ashamed to wear his prison bifocals and he can't put one leg in front of another because guys have been abusing him because of his bad habit.

In prison, everybody has a "word" on you. Well the word on Blanco is that he likes to borrow and not pay back. That's not only a bad habit, it's a deadly prescription, (especially in here) because you can only run for so long before you run into some homies. "Homies," Dad, meaning the opposition of what you *think* you stand for. In other words, the "*other* gang." Well, Dad, this menace to society can tell me how to load every gun available to these cowards, but put a mop in his hand and he's shooting blanks.

Blanco's job is to mop the floor of the tier. My morning job is to make sure the floor gets mopped correctly, because it's my turn to be the Tier Sanitation King. My issue with his mopping stems from what you taught me a long time ago, Daddy. You would always say, "Whether you're mopping a floor or conquering the world, take pride in it and do it right!"

So as every other inmate watched this mop kick Blanco's behind, I stepped in and showed him what "someone" should have showed him 15 years ago. Dip the mop in clean water and Clorox, ring it out, and while applying pressure, move the mop evenly across every square inch of the floor. Don't leave any dry spots and be sure you "don't just wet the floor, son." Water by itself doesn't clean anything, friction does.

Remember how we use to be amazed at our car wash when there was a demand was for a touch-less car wash? No brushes, just water and suds. And what a surprise! As soon as they drove off the other lot and the car dried, it was dirtier than it was before they arrived. Hey, it wasn't such a bad thing because they only came over to our shop and we washed it again for them by hand for $10.95! LOL. Wow.

When other dads were on a ladder fixing the roof and their son would ask, "Daddy, what are you doing up there?" The father would yell, "Get away from here

Up The Ladder

before you get hurt! Plus, can't you see I'm busy!?" Not you, Dad. You took the time to walk down the ladder, then walk me back up the ladder and onto the roof so you could explain what you were fixing. It's a lesson that has stuck with me to this day.

"Learn how things work and then work them!" You used to proudly say, even though I know you were also thinking, *If I don't show this boy how to use this ladder and hammer the right way, he's going to attempt it anyway and hurt himself.*

Either way, Daddy, thanks.

Well, not only has the combination of the Department of Corrections, poor parenting, and the computer age just about eliminated the blue-collar skilled worker, it is also killing its own industry in the process. But a computer can't actually build a prison, right? You need friction, and only human hands can apply this friction.

So why not teach Blanco how to build his own prison? At least he would have a job and the self-esteem that goes along with having one. But realistically, it will likely bring him right back to jail, because without God, it seems almost too late for him to find a father figure to take him up that ladder. Like you always said, Daddy, *You can put all the lipstick you want on a pig, and it's still a pig.*

Daddy, you were never prejudiced, but you never wanted to see a Mexican bricklayer. You knew that if the Spanish started laying bricks, it could potentially flood the market with skilled workers, bring down the price, and possibly run us blacks out of business. I wonder what you think now looking down on me from Heaven into this prison and seeing so many "blancos," not laying bricks, but confined to cages. Wasted talent, right? We could shut the borders if we trained our own "throw away people" to become specialists. You always taught me that a specialist is someone who invests in mastering the thing that someone else either doesn't want to do, or doesn't want to take the time to learn how to do.

Daddy, I'm tired. So tired of slowing up to let these prisoners stay within 100 yards of me, but I can't think like that anymore. I'm going to do what you and God would want me to do. One, bring Blanco up that ladder to the roof and then out on top of the building; while we're there, might as well introduce him to Jesus! Because Daddy, no ladder can bring you to Heaven if you can't answer a simple question correctly. And it all comes down to the question God will ask each one of us, "What did you do with my Son?"

Love you, Daddy,
Jayson

P.S. Daddy, I'm in prison 24 hours a day with the CEO of one of the biggest corporations in the world who molested his own 8- and 10-year-old children. He is Harvard educated and doesn't know how to mop a floor. He even manipulated another comrade to help him sweep. Imagine that! Two grown men sweeping one 6x8 floor. Now, tell me what would happen if he stopped by his corporation one day and noticed two able-bodied individuals doing the work half a man should be doing. Someone would be out of a job, for sure.

Balance, Dad. Balance. Thank you for my college education!

Miss you,
JW

Super Mario

Today in our daily prison Bible study I was terribly confused because I once again tried to please everyone in the fellowship. Man, Dad, I backslid trying to please man. The funny thing is that 30 out of 38 hardened prisoners who attend, there is only one dude who thinks that although I'm rich and famous (or now infamous), I should never talk about it. I call him Mario, because he's a little man who looks like one of the Super Mario Brothers from the video game.

Mario has a friend on our tier who is also a Christian, but he doesn't attend the Fellowship because his ego is too large and he has to be in charge. So he stays on his bunk and puts on his earplugs whenever we have Bible study. Each time I begin to reflect on how I abused the blessings God bestowed on me prior to prison, he starts making faces. First of all, how can he hear me if he's wearing earplugs? LOL.

Peter Marshall says, "Lord, when we are wrong make us willing to change, and when we are right, make us easy to live with." Well then, Dad, I hope I'm easy to live with.

Today we were studying Agur in Proverbs 30:8-9. *"First, help me never to tell a lie. Second, give me neither poverty nor riches! Give me just enough to satisfy my needs. For if I grow rich I may deny You, and say, 'Who is the Lord?' And if I am too poor, I may steal and thus insult God's holy name."* This has become my favorite proverb because I can relate in many ways. But in order to set up my testimony, I would have to talk about fame and fortune. I glanced over my shoulder and saw Mario, and that was it—I missed my mark. I know I could've nailed it and hopefully made a difference in the lives of some of my fellow inmates. Not because they are destined to be rich (maybe), but because my story could teach them to count their blessings and be content with what they have, like I should have been. That would have been such an easy message for me, but I got bamboozled by the mini-me Italian guy who didn't want me to be me because it might offend his big, black, bald-headed friend with the earplugs.

Dad, God's not changing my personality, he's changing my personality flaws. Agur is right up my alley and I wanted to share how God's blessings drove me farther from Him, but only because I misused them. Each time God blessed me with something good, it took the focus off of Him. So the more God blessed me, the more self-absorbed I became. I was stupid enough to think my charity work, donations, and causes gave me the right to tell God to look the other way. Heck, God only gave me 100 million dollars because He killed my three sisters. That's what I thought before he isolated me in a prison with just Him.

"Why does it take prison for people to find God?" Dad, people say this all the time with a skeptical, smug look on their face.

I wanna tell them, "Well, Fool, because you are in an environment where no one else can help you—that's why. I came to prison knowing I was two phone calls away from anyone in the world, yet with as much fame and fortune as I had, no one but God could aid or comfort me. That's why you find God!"

Okay, Dad. Back to the message I delivered very inconsistently because I'm a coward. People used to tell me that they would gladly give their whole life to be me. Well, I did give my whole life to be me — tens of thousands of basketball practices with no vacations or weekends off. But despite everything I had, I was still never content or at peace. Had Super Mario not intimidated me, I probably would have shared my story, but without apologizing or feeling guilty about my fame and fortune. I worked hard, Dad. Does this mean I think a basketball player should be paid more than a fireman, policeman, or teacher? NO! But I have always given to those people and their organizations, even if it was because I felt guilty about my success.

Dad, I will not let anyone alter a testimony I'm giving for God. Never. I just wanted to tell our group what James Stuart Bell's devotional said about the subject. Having too much can cause problems. Agur wrote in Proverbs that the rich tend to be self-sufficient, self indulgent, and self-satisfied; and such people (like me) easily forget their need for God. Agur also saw dangerous pitfalls in poverty and worried that if things got desperate enough, he might do foolish things that would dishonor himself and God. Agur advised his readers to have just enough to feel satisfied, but not so much that they neglect their Provider.

Dad, any weakness—like being a coward for God and changing my testimony to soothe envious people—is unacceptable. Weakness I refuse to deal with. It will draw me toward the wrong things and set me up for defeat. To live victoriously I must recognize that.

I love you, Dad!
Jayson

Hope

All that is gold does not glitter,
Not all those who wander are lost;
The old that is strong does not wither, Deep roots are not reached by the frost.

From the ashes a fire shall be woken, A light from the shadows shall spring; Renewed shall be blade that was broken, The crownless again shall be king.

~ J.R.R. Tolkien, *The Fellowship of the Ring*

Dad,

This morning I read something that scared me. It said, "Everything we ever hope in will eventually let us down." Is that true? Does it always turn out that way? Dad, my hope is in God—I know He won't let me down—but is that true? Will every other hope eventually break my heart? Maybe I'm just worried that I will disappoint, too. That I will let everyone down again. Now I see why women go crazy when we don't communicate and ignore them. It's the *not knowing* that drives them crazy.

Danny, a fellow inmate, came home from work and found his best friend sleeping with his wife and killed them both. It was a crime of passion. His impulsive reaction landed him in prison for 20 years to life. I wonder if Dan knew then what he knows now, would he have

Hope

done it anyway? I don't know. Danny is a 5'7", 135 lb. white man who came to prison not knowing much, but now knows more than anyone should ever care to know. Because of his stature and inexperience, Dan was raped multiple times by various inmates throughout the years. This is what happens, Dad. It's disturbing, but it happens. A larger, more intimidating inmate will offer the smaller, less-imposing inmates protection from the evils of prison. But the "protected" becomes property of the "protector." Sad, but true. I've heard countless stories like this. No inmate would hope for a prison experience like this. But it happens, Dad.

So after 20 years of this and other unknowns, Dan had his day with parole. He has been turned down every year for 10 years and is now on his 31st year in prison. I'm scared to have an opinion about Danny's debt to society, but I will tell you what I've seen from him. Danny is always smiling and always jovial. I see him in church, but Danny is best known for his running. Danny is the Forrest Gump of the NJ prison system because he runs and he runs and he runs. I run too, Dad, but not like Danny. I wonder what he's thinking as he runs each lap past 20 feet of barbed-wire fences in a yard lined with constant reminders that you are a prisoner of the state. But Danny doesn't run like that. Danny runs like he is a prisoner of hope. What keeps Danny running? Day after day, and year after year, what goes through his head?

You left for Heaven on November 10, 2009. Would you have wanted to know that date ahead of time? Would it have made a difference? Do we need to know these things? After Linda died of AIDS, you and Mom saw how sad I was. So when Laura was sick, you said it was liver disease. After she died, I found out it was AIDS. Would I have been better off knowing the truth? Or would knowing be worse? I might have missed out on those last days, weeks, and months with her had

I known—or maybe not. Do we want to know these things? Do we need to know when and why marriages go bad, or when and why tragedy will strike?

So Danny keeps running. He runs and he runs and he runs, as if his prison release depends on it. His hope must rise and fall year after year as parole passes him by. He does not know when prison will end—or if he will ever see the outside—but he runs as though he does. He runs like he's preparing for freedom. He runs with hope.

I guess we are all just prisoners of hope. I can't tell you what Dan is thinking or what he hopes in, or if he hopes at all. But something makes this man press forward. There is something else in his life that keeps him going. One thing I do know, Dad, thanks to Danny. I've gotta hang on to hope. I've gotta keep running with hope.

Miss you, Daddy,
Jayson

P.S. *"He gives power to the weak and strength to the powerless. Even youths will become weak and tired, and young men will fall in exhaustion. But those who hope in the Lord will find new strength. They will soar high on wings like eagles. They will run and not grow weary. They will walk and not faint."* Isaiah 40:29-31

Cursing

Dear Dad,

Just a real quick note to you today. First of all, I love you and miss you. Now that I have buttered you all up, I slipped up yesterday.

Mike H., a 6' 3", 300 lb white guy who likes to be called "White Mike", rejected my offer to come to church last night. Then, White Mike, okay, just Mike, started blaspheming church and God. He wanted me to show him where in the Bible does it say a man can't do drugs to get high. I could've told him to go to 1 Corinthians 3:16-17, about the body being a temple, but I just went short and blunt. "Mike, anything that separates you from God, like drunkenness, is not acceptable."

Mike became anal and aggressive. Now Daddy, I have completely stopped cursing, thanks to Matt's coaching, but I did call Mike an ignorant cracker who tries to make the Bible fit his vices. "West Coast", a white inmate in his 31st year, overheard my comment and was offended by it, even though I said it jokingly. He told me that he was disappointed in a Christian using that kind of language, even in prison.

Dad, West Coast hadn't been to church in 30 years until the day I invited him, and he hasn't missed a Sunday since. So, I rushed to explain to West Coast that this behavior was not racist, just asinine. He agreed, knowing my mother is white and that I've always gotten along with all races in this prison. "Jayson, you are the only Bible I have ever trusted, so don't let me down again."

"No problem, West Coast. It won't happen again," I said as I stared at the swastika on his forehead.

Remember Dad, this was the same man who was going to cut Matt's throat while he slept. Oh yeah, did I mention he's serving his 31st year? Dad, to whom much is given, much is required. So I must be careful— no, I must not do these things anymore, period. I was wrong and it won't happen anymore.

Dad, do you remember when your grandson Isaac was three years old and he cursed in church? Reverend Tremble stopped preaching and you picked Isaac up, threw him over your shoulder, and then marched toward the exit past a dead silent congregation. Then suddenly, Isaac, knowing his faith, looked back at the preacher and shouted, "Pray for me! Pray for me!"

I remember that day, LOL.

Hold on, Dad. As I'm writing this not-so-quick letter, West Coast (who is obviously okay with me now), just told me he had a parrot 35 years ago. This parrot used to curse up a storm and he tried everything to stop this behavior, from shaking the cage, to putting a blanket over the cage, but the parrot would still shout out curses.

So one day, he had enough and put the parrot in the freezer. The parrot kicked and cursed and then there was silence. Now Dad, don't forget who is telling me this story and where we are, and how vulnerable my neck is. So he gets 100% of my attention.

West Coast says, "So it's been a few minutes and fearing the parrot may have frozen to death, I opened the freezer door. The parrot calmly stepped out into my outstretched arms and said, 'I believe I may have offended you with my rude language and actions. I'm sincerely remorseful for my inappropriate transgressions, and I fully intend to everything I can to correct my rude and unforgivable behavior.'"

West Coast was stunned at the change in the bird's attitude. As he was about to ask the parrot what had made such a dramatic change in his behavior, the bird continued. "May I ask what the turkey did?"

Daddy, then we hugged in laughter. (I was more frisking him and searching him for a shank. I don't need to hear *me* go thump in the night.) Just another example of communicate, then forgive, forget, and laugh. We always have interesting days in here, but today was funny and I thank God for that.

Love you Big Daddy,
J

Sleep Conversations

Dear Dad,

It's 2:40 a.m. and this letter will be short and straight to the point because I'm not supposed to be using light to do anything at this hour. Come to think of it, this is when I typically get into the most trouble. The big difference is I'm sober now, 336 days straight. Nothing good happens after midnight, like you said.

This is when the inmates have their nightmares—another reason I don't want to stay awake. Like right now. I'm in hell, Dad! One minute the coward is snoring, the next he is rambling about twisted crimes—without ever turning on his cot. Satan and his soldiers come here at night. Makes me wonder if these monsters can be rehabilitated? They're killing in their sleep, Dad, and worse.

They joke, then threaten, then kill with their eyes closed and half a smile on their faces. The most evil and straight-from-the-center-of-hell criminals damage innocent children. Innocent kids crying out—trapped in the dreams of my filthy neighbors. Satan's dormitory and playground—open while the rest of the world sleeps.

Just a minute ago I heard a child being told, "Go ahead! Yell louder, no one can help you!" Followed by a sinister, mocking laugh and more mumbling. Then, Satan himself whispers, then sneers, "You can keep screaming as loud as you want and it don't matter. I don't care how loud you scream. No one will ever hear you!"

One guy is commanding an army, the next guy is crying for protection, and another inmate is raping and murdering—only to be interrupted by an inmate a couple bunks away screaming profanities at his mother. Now tell me, how am I supposed to greet these guys in the mess hall five hours from now?

Dad, this is serious! I'm in hell! The scariest thing of all is that by morning, they carry on like usual. No remorse.

God help me and keep me!
J

Let Sydney Sing

Dear Dad,

After 17 years in prison, Sydney, a 6'3" 300 lb. African American man with a smile only a vampire can love, is leaving to go home. After attending church in prison religiously, he only has one request. He wants to sing a song of praise and worship to the prison church. Now to me, singing is basically a form of pleasant, controlled screaming. The problem is that the preacher with the Napoleon Complex doesn't want to be outshined. Now, I'm not calling the preacher "Satan," (not yet, anyway) but Satan will try to steal the joy of service in two ways:

1. He wants us to compare ourselves to one another.
2. He wants to get us to conform our ways to the expectations of others.

The Bible warns us never to compare ourselves to others. Do your own work well, and then you will have something to be proud of. But don't compare yourself with others.

Two reasons:

1. You will likely find someone doing a better job than you, and you will become discouraged.

2. You will always be able to find someone who doesn't seem as effective as you, and you will become full of pride.

So, Dad, I hope this jailhouse preacher understands this and lets Sydney sing tonight. I hope he listens to God's voice. The old Jay might have tried to use "God's megaphone" to get this accomplished, but not anymore.

Love you, Daddy!
JW

P.S. "Let Sydney Sing" ~ GOD

Rich or Poor?

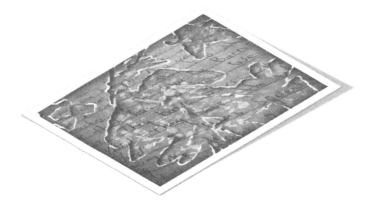

Dear Dad,

As we were coming up on the holidays here in prison, you can actually see depression setting in amongst the inmates. Altercations are more readily available.

To go out or eat in...

There will be no visits today on Christmas, the Warden just announced this personally. Not that my daughters were planning to come see me anyway. But if they were, it would automatically be a double-edged sword. *Spend the day with Jesus and opening your presents*, is my first thought. Who would wish prison on anyone—especially children, and especially on Christmas? But what if it's not about what I want? What if they really did want to see me? Then it's just me being selfish again. I'm bewildered once more and have decided to go on another fast for spiritual clarity.

Lon, another Christian, showed me a great Christmas card. It was Santa Claus going into church wishing Jesus Happy Birthday. Non-Christians in here didn't understand it, so I tried to explain it to them, but to no avail.

As I was trying to explain the real significance of Christmas, our jailhouse preacher told me sarcastically, "Jayson you can lead a horse to water, but you can't make him drink."

Thinking to myself, *Explaining Jesus is supposed to be YOUR job,* I snapped back, "Let me give you some advice. My job is not to make the horse drink, it's to make him thirsty."

Moving on...

Christmas carols, anyone?

Anyway, I remember you and I rarely shared Christmas gifts. Then there was that one year when I was feeling a little too good about my financial status and I said to you in front of my mansion, "Don't get me anything for Christmas, because what can you get a man who has everything?"

You didn't like that comment and drove away looking disappointed. After a couple days, you returned and told me that you broke down in West Virginia on a rural road. You said you walked three miles to a farm. It was a very poor farm and you had to ask for help.

The gracious family invited you in for lunch and you spent the afternoon exchanging stories about our farm. I remember asking you, "Dad, do you see how poor we used to be before the NBA? Do you remember that?"

You answered, "I saw that we have a cat and those people that welcomed me had three. I saw that we have a pool that reaches all the way to the barn, they have a creek that has no end. We have fancy lamps in our mansion, they have stars. Our balcony reaches to the front yard, they have the whole horizon. I saw that they were grateful, godly people."

Dad when you were finished, I was speechless, then you added, "Thanks, Son, for reminding me how poor we are!" We always understood each other when we spoke in parables like that. This Christmas I'm the wealthiest man alive because I have Jesus. Really, Dad, I have Jesus.

   Merry Christmas, Daddy.
   I love you and forgive me for being an idiot.
   J

Merry Christmas!

Merry Christmas, Daddy!

I wrote in my first book, *Loose Balls*, about how Mommy's sister Gerry made me sleep on the porch with all the fishing poles and the dirty smelly linen and all I had was Dutchess, their dog, to keep me company. The night was frigid. I was seven years old and I remember crying because I thought they put me out there by myself because I must smell or something. As I petted Dutchess, the door opened and I thought I was going to be saved and brought into the warmth of Aunt Gerry's home.

"Dutchess! Get in here!" Aunt Gerry shouted. "Come, boy, come on into the house!" Then the door slammed and I turned over on the fishhook-infested, oily couch and cried for you to come save me.

Well Dad, when Aunt Gerry read this she was very upset and thought about suing me. About a year later, she talked to her oldest son Frankie and he corroborated my story. Aunt Gerry apologized to me some 30-odd years later. She explained that she loved me and always took me in when you and Mommy were not, let's say, having the best of times. I believed her.

Now as I lay in my cell Dad, can you believe that because of all the tragedies in my childhood, the only Christmas I can honestly remember is when I was at Aunt Gerry and Uncle Mike's house in Brooklyn when I was five years old? They woke me up with the rest of my cousins on Christmas morning and gave me a Batmobile that had lights and bounced into walls and went in different directions. Well, I guess it went in different directions, or maybe I helped it.

I can remember the tree in the corner, the egg white colored walls and the TV with the record player on top—a one-piece entertainment center. I was wearing yellow Donald Duck pajamas, no—Winnie the Pooh, the kind with the footsies in them.

Daddy, I hurt Aunt Gerry and even embarrassed her. She loved me because I was always over their house. Dang, how many "not so good times" did you and Mom have?

What's more amazing? I would have never remembered this important cut in my life or realized that now—35 years later—part of me still hasn't healed.

Time doesn't heal everything—God does! God showed me how Aunt Gerry loved me and how much I love her.

Merry Christmas, Daddy!
J

No Angel

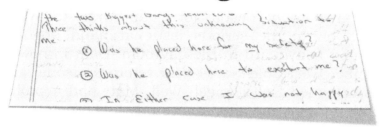

> There is no use whatsoever trying to help people who do not help themselves. You cannot push anyone up a ladder unless he be willing to climb himself.
> ~ Andrew Carnegie

Dear Dad,

Another inmate we tried to help, let's just call him Midnite, was a gang member stationed next to my bunk by the head of one of the two biggest gang leaders (O.G. = original gangsta). There are three things about this unknown situation that troubled me:
 1. Was Midnite placed here for my safety?
 2. Was he placed here to extort me?
 3. In either case, I was not happy about this because any gang member, even the Mafia, I consider an agent of genocide to our communities.

Midnite was an interesting character to me. He was a large man in pretty good shape, but very quiet. He was slow to speak, unless he was begging. Then, of course, he sounded like an auctioneer. *I need one cigarette, two cigarettes, three. Who will give me two cigarettes now or I will kill you! Sold! To the lil' old white man, C.E.O! You get to see tomorrow.* I often thought about what you always said, "Better to beg than steal, but better to work than beg." So I always gave him stuff, mainly because I was a sucker for his story, which was like molasses moving in the wintertime, slow and boring. Plus, he was like the guy on Popeye, Wimpy, who always said, "I will gladly pay you on Tuesday for a hamburger today."

Well, on to the serious issue at hand about my unwanted bodyguard in the dayroom. Dad, I know you remember West Coast, a 34-year veteran prisoner and a self-proclaimed Hell's Angel. Well, Matt had a problem with West Coast and after an argument between the two, Matt went on about his Bible study while West Coast started suiting up like Rambo. Now West Coast already looks like Charles Manson, but when he started putting his wall locks in a sock and sharpening his tools, I thought about going to talk to him myself, but that could make things worse and send the wrong message. Matt is a grown man and capable of cleaning up his own mess, with this loner anyway. So I sent Midnite back there to diffuse the situation and he did. He lived up to his reputation.

But Midnite had another reputation, one of being demonically possessed. He would lie on his bunk all night and wrestle outwardly with Satan. Wow. It was a sight to see. A slow-moving demonically possessed, begging gang member. Wow. Midnite would sometimes win and grab the demon by the throat and throw him on the next person who walked by, and that person, too scared to address Midnite, would run to Holy Joe or open his Bible. One way or another, God will get you to open your Bible. He does work in mysterious ways. LOL.

Well, Midnite asked me for a job as a crane operator at my construction job. I can only imagine watching Midnite trying to place a skid of blocks on a scaffold six stories in the air and then suddenly having a demonic attack, or jumping off the crane in mid-action to beg for a smoke, which he would gladly pay you back for on Tuesday.

Dad, I know from past experiences with the devil that he is alive and hungry. So I tried to shake my shadow whenever I could or just give him a smoke so he would go away. Better a smoke than my soul.

Dad, I didn't wrestle with my gift of discernment for long because Midnite was released on Thursday and I saw him again on the Saturday morning news, charged with murder in the first degree. While he was being placed in the car, based on my few similar experiences, I imagined the policeman was saying, "Watch your head," as Midnite ducked into the back seat. Or he could have been saying, "No, dude, I don't have a smoke."

Daddy, I usually would be kicking myself in the rear right now because I would be thinking I could have saved him. But I'm not. He's not Jacob and that was no angel he was wrestling with.

Enough said.

I love you, Dad,

J

P.S. Turns out Midnite killed a corrections officer. It was a revenge shooting against a CO who shot another gang member in 2007.

Simple Solution

Dear Dad,

Today I'm kind of all over the place. I have a visit in a little bit with former NETS president Michael Rowe. You and Mike had a great relationship—especially since he put 86 million dollars in our account. Dad, I'm bewildered because I'm disappointed in what I have to tell you in this letter.

Dad, do you remember me telling you about Mr. Murphy, the 67-year-old gentleman who sings in the prison church choir? He's the guy who committed 106 robberies in his signature pink Bugs Bunny costume, using a shotgun and a.45 pistol. He started off each robbery by firing one shotgun blast over the clerk's head into the can of pork and beans or whatever he saw on the shelf that would make the biggest mess.

Well, anyway Dad, I've been eager to pick his brain ever since I met him, mainly because he's been in the system since the '60s, if not before. Last night he spoke

Simple Solution

with Matt and I for at least an hour and told maybe a dozen stories, a couple of them were especially disturbing. Like his thoughts on gay sex in prison and the DOC. Mr. Murphy said that from 1964 to 1972, during his time at another state prison, the Department of Corrections subtly encouraged gay sex. They turned a blind eye to gay marriages, figuring that bringing a gay lover behind the walls might help calm unruly inmates and establish good behavior incentives for "lifers" with triple life sentences and no ties to the outside. If the inmate got out of line, his "wife" was moved to another part of the prison. According to Mr. Murphy, this method of punishment worked for the most part, unless the wife cheated. Then all hell would break loose. He told me a story about a white inmate, a self-proclaimed racist, who fell in love with a black inmate and both were "married" within the walls of state prison. The racist warned all the other prisoners that his wife, "Satin Doll," was off-limits. Three black inmates missed that memo and the racist slit each of their throats in retaliation. He wrote a letter to the Warden explaining his actions, quoting a phrase that has long been attributed to Mark Twain, "I did not attend their funerals, but I wrote a nice letter saying I approved of them."

Mr. Murphy also told me about something alarming that he personally witnessed over 100 times when he was a free man. He watched ladies, young African queens, take their little five and six-year-old daughters, their princesses, our princesses, to be sold into prostitution for as little as five dollars. Dad, this is definitely a problem. What substance is worth the price of your baby's innocence? For a high? This is serious stuff. What has the world come to?

I wanted solutions. "So how can we stop the gang violence in our communities?"

"That's easy," he said, "The electric chair. These young kids today view prison a reasonable alternative to life on the streets. It's all about self-preservation. These young gang members are forced to take orders from their captains and when given the option to kill or be killed, they kill. They kill so they can go to prison and live."

I asked this old-timer every question I could think of about prison, gangs, their families, their motives, a ton of questions. I was impressed with his take on what goes on in the minds of the criminal, the OG, the "prison wife," and even the DOC. He's seen it all, Dad. Finally, I hit him with the ultimate question, "So what do we have to do to stop them from joining gangs in the first place, or once in prison, get out of that lifestyle?"

Mr. Murphy looked at us as though we should already know the answer. The solution was simple, according to him.

"God. They need to put God in their lives. Nothing else can be done."

After Mr. Harris said that he got up and stirred the rice in his bowl, then left our presence like he just realized that he wasted over an hour of his life explaining "life" to two more people who can't or won't make a difference.

Gotta go see Mr. Rowe, Dad.

Bye!

J

Shake It Off!

Dear Dad,

I was telling some of the inmates about the parable that our family used to share with me after I had bad games. In prison, the main game is to survive. Never let them see you with your head down. Don't allow anyone to make you answer your adversity with self-pity or bitterness. Respond positively and trust in God.

Just like the story of the mule who fell in the well.

The mule fell into the farmer's well. The farmer heard the mule "braying," or whatever mules do when they fall into a well. After carefully assessing the situation, the farmer sympathized with the mule, but decided that neither the mule nor the well was worth the trouble of saving. Instead, he called a couple of farmers together and explained the situation. He asked them to help him haul some dirt to bury the old stubborn mule in the well and put him out of his misery.

Initially, the mule was hysterical! But as the farmer

and his neighbors continued shoveling and heaving the dirt into the well and onto the mule's back, it suddenly dawned on him: every time a shovel load of dirt landed on his back, he would just shake if off and step up! And that is exactly what the stubborn old mule did. Shovel load by shovel load, *shake it off and step up.*

Shake it off and step up! He kept repeating to himself. No matter how painful the loads of shovel were, or how stressful and gloomy the situation seemed, the old mule fought the panic and anxiety and just kept shaking it off and stepping up!

It wasn't long before the old mule, tired and beat up, stepped triumphantly out of that well. What seemed like it would bury him actually helped him, all because of how this old mule handled his adversity.

I need to read this letter more often, Daddy.

Love you,
Jayson

Take Heed

Let me first give you the scriptures before I give you my observations from prison.

John 12:8, *"For the poor you have with you always, but Me you do not have always."*

John 12:35-36, *"Then Jesus said to them, A little while longer the light is with you. Walk while you have the light, lest darkness overtake you."*

I truly believe Jesus is giving us inmates an offer we can't refuse. Jesus put us here to give us a final choice to walk with Him or not.

For myself, I spent so much time preparing for this life here on earth. All the cars, houses, more cars, jewelry, clothes, women, etc., but I never took even the slightest amount of time to think about Eternity.

My daddy used to have his own way of deciphering a Bible verse. He did the same thing with music. I would ask him to repeat a rap song from Jay Z and he would take one word of the rap and make the rest up himself. It would mean the same thing, but with fewer words.

Dad would always say, "Man that comes from a woman, life is but a vapor." Well, the sentence that the judge ordered me to serve in prison isn't even a vapor compared to my human life. God must have wanted to use this time to show me how great it is to have Him right now in "prison"— prison being my earthly life. He had to put me in a grown-up time-out to show me how much He loves me.

Walk while you have the light. Take heed, Jayson, and stay in the light, lest the darkness overtake you.

Do I want to be with my family on the other side of the wall (which is Heaven in earthly terms), or do I want to spend the rest of my life doing nothing in here? God is giving me this opportunity to slow down and enjoy Him, to see if I really love Him. If I do, I can have Him forever.

Being an earthly superstar preoccupied all my time. Very rarely did I focus on what it takes to be with the greatest Superstar, forever.

I could just end it here, but I want to remind myself to read this again when I'm released and about to slip into darkness.

Thank you, God, for this observation.

Do-Over

Dear Dad,

Today is a reflective day. Another inmate who was reading *Loose Balls* showed me a passage in the book where I said when I want to be remembered as a good son and father after I die, and that I want people to remember me as a good friend. Today I had a change of heart. But before I changed my epitaph, I asked a couple of my fellow inmates what they wanted to hear people say when they see them lying there in a casket at their funeral.

Brother Rice says, "I would like to hear them say that I was a great cop who made one bad mistake, and I'm a family man."

The second prisoner, Holy Joe says, "I would like to hear that I was a wonderful husband and pastor who made a change."

With my new prison mentality, I replied, "I would like to hear them say, 'Look! Jay's moving!'"

If I were to die today, I would need a do-over, Dad. But if God let's me see the second half, I will make you proud again.

Love you,
Jay

Planted

"And he shall be like a tree planted by the rivers of water, that brings forth its fruit in its season; his leaf also shall not wither; and whatsoever he does shall prosper."
Psalm 1:3

Dear Daddy, ☺

To protect themselves from the enemy from the north, the people of China built the Great Wall. It was so high nobody could climb over it and so thick nobody could break through it, so they settled back to enjoy life. During the first 100 years of the wall's existence, China was invaded three times. Not once did the enemy try to break down the wall or climb over it, they simply bribed the gatekeeper and marched in.

Those who built it were relying on the stone wall to protect them. Meanwhile, they neglected to teach integrity to their children. As a result, they grew up without moral and spiritual principles to guide them. Dad, our family is comprised of storytellers and I learned most of my values from the stories that have been passed down for generations. Well, here goes another one. I read this today and hope you enjoy it.

A mighty wind blew night and day. It stole the oak tree's leaves away, then snapped its branches and pulled its bark, until the oak was tired and empty. But still the oak tree held its ground while other trees fell all around. The fierce wind gave up and spoke, "How can you still be standing, Oak?"

The oak tree said, "I know that you can break each branch of mine in two, carry every leaf away, shake my limbs, and make me sway. But I have roots stretched in the earth, growing stronger since my birth. You'll never touch them for you see, they are the deepest part of me. Until today, I wasn't sure of just how much I could endure. But now I've found with thanks to you, I'm stronger than I ever knew.

Dad, this is exactly the type of integrity you instilled in me as a child. But I lost my way when I decided to make Jesus my co-pilot.

So now, I must regularly ask myself: Am I the same no matter who I'm with? Am I willing to make decisions that are best for others, even though another choice would benefit me more? Can I be counted on this time to keep the commitments I've made to God and you, Dad? I didn't before. But just like an alcoholic, I must take it one day at a time. I must have high self-esteem at all times so that I don't jeopardize my integrity.

I also must watch the trees that are planted around me. Dad, in the South you used to tell me about the "southern weed"—the pine tree. They are everywhere and most times they impede the sun's rays on a beautiful oak, causing the oak tree to have to bend and reform to attract some sun. If I don't surround myself with weeds, I won't have to conform or modify myself just to get closer to the sun—the sun being God. I am an oak, Dad, planted by the water, and I cannot be moved.

You are my roots, "Big Daddy."

Love you,
Jayson

CPSIA information can be obtained at www.ICGtesting.com
Printed in the USA
BVOW11s0145270814

364376BV00026B/432/P

9 781622 304639